WHAT NEVER LEAVES

DANIEL TAM-CLAIBORNE

For Oberlin Shansi

In loving memory
Jon Kawano (1955 – 2011)

Published by Wilder Voice Books
Wilder Voice Books is an imprint of Wilder Voice Press
Cover image by Jennifer Wu

Second printing: May, 2014
Printed in the United States of America

PUBLISHER'S NOTE
This book is based on some true events; however, it has been fictionalized. Names, characters, places, and
incidents are either the product of the author's imagination or are used fictitiously, and any resemblance to
actual persons, living or dead, business establishments, events, or locales is entirely coincidental.

WILDER VOICE BOOKS

Is a small division of Wilder Voice Press, which prints a reasonably-sized magazine called *Wilder Voice*
twice a year in Oberlin, OH. The photograph that appears on the front cover was taken by Jennifer
Wu and is of the Shanxi Agricultural University Market—a place about which you can read in this
very book! Wilder Voice Press is comprised of a small staff of reasonably-reasonable people: John West,
President; Emily Kennedy, Senior Vice-President; David Ohana, Vice President for Finance and Business
Development; Allison Fontaine-Capel, Artistic Director. Wilder Voice Books: John West, Editor-in-Chief;
Emily Kennedy, Managing Editor; Sage Aronson, Senior Associate Editor; Kara Kralik, Associate Editor.
We are indebted to the League of Moveable Type for League Gothic and Raleway, two beautiful, open-
source display fonts used in this book. We also use Adobe Garamond Pro, naturally. Paperback editions
of this book are expertly printed by Bodnar Printing Company in Lorain, Ohio, through Oberlin College
printing services in Oberlin, OH—thanks to Wendy. No, really, thanks to Wendy. Feel free to direct any
questions, comments, curio, or courtesy straws to wildervoice@wildervoice.org. We also have a website.
It is situated at http://wildervoice.org. The names 'Wilder Voice,' Wilder Voice Press,' and 'Wilder Voice
Books' are all trademarks of Wilder Voice Press, which is in no way affiliated with Wilder Hall or the
Oberlin College Wilder Student Union. It's all right; we're not wild about them either.

WHAT NEVER LEAVES

SETTLING IN

REJECTION

DESPAIR

EDITOR'S NOTE

I first met Dan at a bowling league, but the transition from bowling partner to editor did not take place until some years later.

Dan's bowling shot is not traditional. He starts with poise, cool and calm. Then, with almost cartoonish strides, he lurches down the approach only to place the ball down gently on the lane.

Dan's proposal was elegant and exciting, and the editorial staff accepted it immediately. At my first meeting with Dan, I was reminded again of his understated cool. He had some blog and journal entries that he was working from, and, all in all, he seemed to have a surprisingly clear perspective on his two-year stint in rural China. By our next meeting, only a week later, Dan had written 50 pages, thought of two ideas for a title, picked out pictures for the cover, shifted briefly to the third-person, and introduced over a dozen characters. We were now in the approach.

As the weeks progressed, Dan's ideas multiplied—each one giving rise to its own unique set of implications and perspectives. I was reminded of Borges's short story "The Garden of Forking Paths" and the fractal-like progression toward infinite possibilities. Narrative arcs would rise and reach their apex somewhere in the confines of Dan's mind—which, while assumedly a fanciful place, remained largely inaccessible to his editor.

After six months, Dan had nearly 80,000 words. He came into the meeting informing me that it was reaching the length of the first *Twilight* book, and that he wanted to stop so as to not draw any unwanted comparisons. At this point, I had read every word, never in the intended order, and, while I had a sense of the overall effect of the book, the emergent themes and tone were largely a mystery. So, when I sat down to read the first complete draft, I was nervous as to what I would find.

It was a smooth read—surprising for a rough draft. Toward the end, I observed that the innumerable themes and arcs—that I had, up until this point, lost track of in the mystique of Dan's mind—had come full circle. Reading the final page, I realized that Dan, with his frenetic, cartoonish approach, had done exactly what he had sought out to do. With his lurching genius, he had created something truly unique.

The following manuscript is a genre-defying piece of creative nonfiction. It is part travel writing and part memoir. Though, on second thought, it is really none of these things. Dan is sometimes the protagonist and sometimes the fly on the wall. He is sometimes a tourist and sometimes a local. He is a teacher and a student—a confident Casanova and a meek twenty-something that finds himself way over his head.

This manuscript follows the seven stages of culture shock, with each book relating to a different stage. Each book is further broken into several chapters that are self-contained short stories connected to one another by common characters, themes, and quandaries. Without further ado, please enjoy this peek into Dan's mind and his tales from afar.

- Sage Aronson
Senior Associate Editor
Wilder Voice Books

FOREWORD

Before it was the Pacific heir to the American century or home to the world's largest detention of cyber dissidents, China was an apparition lodged in the back of my throat. My mother, whose family fled China during the Second Sino-Japanese War in the mid-twentieth century, grew up in Cuba and moved to America when she was six years old. Over two decades later, I was born, the first of two children, and grew up in a shared, one-bedroom apartment in Brooklyn, New York.

Having only intermittent contact with my American father following my parents' divorce, my childhood was peppered with traditions carried over and dutifully approximated from eight thousand miles away. I woke up each Chinese New Year startled by the sound of firecrackers exploding just beyond our third-floor fire escape. We burned colored paper every autumn in a squat metal tin at the gravestone of the Chinese grandparents I'd never met. Every dinner with extended family ended with a broth of boiled chicken innards, so noxious that I had to hold my nose just to keep down.

My throat knew the contours of those experiences and others—the way they smelled and tasted—at turns salty and bitter, but always distinctly *Chinese*. But at the same time, my throat was speechless. My vocal cords were powerless to replicate the sounds of the Cantonese dialect spoken by my aunts, my cousins, and my own mother. China found its place in my throat but was stuck there, like sticky-sweet *yuanxiao*—round balls of glutinous rice—incapable of being swallowed or spit back up. My connection to China was paradoxical, at once receptive and resisting, familiar and foreign.

As I got older, that connection grew more complex. In high school, I was one of only two Asian Americans in my grade, a distinction that New York City, for all of its diversity, was powerless to help me negotiate. It was not until college that I truly began to embrace my mixed heritage. In the fall of my junior year at Oberlin College, I studied abroad in Osaka, Japan and though I enjoyed my time there, something was missing. More than anything, it exposed me to just how much of the world I had yet to experience.

In my senior year, I decided to take up Mandarin Chinese. It was my attempt at bridging the generational gap between my extended family and me. I felt an instant kinship toward Mandarin, a feeling unlike any I had experienced with other second languages. The rise and fall of the tones set my larynx ablaze: at long last I had found my voice. My relatives met the announcement that I had accepted a Shansi Fellowship to spend the next two years teaching English in China after graduation tepidly. Though they were happy, in some ways they knew, like me, that in two radically different dialects we would still not be able to communicate.

Before I left for China, it struck me that the whole experience would be this life-affirming journey, a chance, after twenty-one years, to finally come to terms with my identity. Pretty soon, however, I discovered that my expectations could not have been more false. The northern Chinese town of Taigu was dilapidated, coal-covered, and mired in poverty. Nearly everything—from the customs to the diet—felt antithetical to the modern-day coastal boom-towns that my grandparents had left behind.

Living in China's rural countryside challenged everything I thought I knew about China. China wasn't confined to my own familial practices nor did it exist solely in splashy, front-page headlines. Never before had I felt so connected to a place, nor to the people who occupied it.

Where I failed to fully grasp my identity, I uncovered something far greater: the untold stories of a country brimming with life and energy, of a ceaselessly evolving landscape. China wasn't merely in my blood; it was so much bigger than myself. When I returned to the United States in August, I went and visited my relatives. Despite the differences in dialect, we exchanged ideas for the first time, writing down the characters that for each of us held the same meaning.

- Daniel Tam-Claiborne
Excerpted from "Why China?" 12/2011

DUNHUANG

MUMBAI

CHIANG MAI

VANG VIENG

ARRIVAL

The first few days in Asia will no doubt be among the most exhilarating of your life. Every taste, smell, and sight will be vivid. You will probably feel that you are learning a great deal—and you are! Confusion about your new environment also will be there, but it won't bother you... yet. You will be able to see your language study bear fruit. You may be able to understand five-year-old speech, sometimes! [†]

[†] Derived from Professor Joseph Elder's notes to University of Wisconsin year abroad program students. Professor Elder was a Shansi Fellow in India from 1953 to 1955.

FALSE STARTS

Two of my bags were missing. Not ten minutes after landing and already there was a crisis. I waited. Ten more minutes passed, then twenty. My body was stiff and I was sweating, my eyes trained to the dark steel chute pushing suitcases and lopsided boxes around the carousel. In reality, this should not have come as a shock. Had I been paying more attention, I would have realized that during my three-hour layover in Beijing I should have retrieved my bags from one set of carousels and checked them back in at another—enduring yet another pat-down search, another emptying of the garbled contents of my pockets, and another polite smile from the airline representative who in her head was doubtless thinking: *Great, another American who can't speak my language.*

In retrospect, the steps were clear. Had I followed them, I might have even spared myself from getting swindled out of 100 *kuai* by a pretty, well-dressed tourist representative fielding questions at the exit gate for confused travelers. Her eyes perked up when I approached.

"How do I get to Tai Yuan?" I tried first in Chinese, readying myself for her response.

"I'm sorry, I don't understand you," she replied in convincing British English.

"Tai Yuan," I repeated, though the rest I tried the second time in English. She thought for a moment.

"Oh, you must mean *Tàiyuán*," she said, correcting me, her upturned finger tracing the second tone in the air. I nodded sheepishly. "I can take you there if you want," she mouthed, her hands at her hips. Already my money was as good as hers, but I could tell even she felt a little guilty about it.

The flight itself was mercifully forgiving, and I slipped through Beijing customs and immigration in short bursts of hazy recall. In the three-hour layover between flights, I bought myself an iced tea, curled up with a Chinese newspaper, and listened intermittently to a TV newscast, reveling in my utter inadequacy. I was unconscious for the entirety of the second flight. It wasn't until the seatbelt lights went off and the passengers next to me started shoving me with their elbows that I realized we had not only left Beijing, but we had already arrived in Taiyuan.

By now, the conveyor belt was empty, and finally, the track stopped moving altogether. I conceded that my bags were not going to emerge in Moses-parting-the-Red-Sea fashion and I would have to speak to one of the airline officials to get the matter straightened out.

The group of concerned friends, relatives, and sign-holding escorts near the baggage claim had by this time thinned to no more than a handful. Each of them had an interest in me regardless of whether or not they actually knew me, and though I didn't know it at the time, theirs were the same wide-eyed, prolonged stares that would soon become a permanent fixture of my existence for the next two years. But one of them in particular held my gaze longer than any of the others. It was clear that he was sent by the Foreign Affairs Office to retrieve me, to do the grunt work of staking out floor space in a dank county airport on a Friday night. From email correspondence, I knew that his name was Li Feng. In the hierarchy of Chinese bureaucracy, he was third on the totem pole—right under Zhao Huang, who was in charge of our teaching schedule, and Xiao Yin, director of the Foreign Affairs Office. He still ranked higher than Rui Wan, the cook and all-purpose helper hired by the school. Li Feng had written to ask me about my scheduled flight arrival and about my visa paperwork. His English was very intelligible and surprisingly fluid.

He was situated on the near side of the railing. If I wanted, I could have reached out and grabbed his hand from my side of the baggage claim; I was surely close enough to exchange a few words. But I didn't. I didn't even go so far as to acknowledge my recognition of him, or my certainty that he-knew-that-I-knew-that-he-knew that I was having some difficulties. I couldn't let this be my lasting first impression, sitcom-like in its absurdity, with the confused foreign teacher having lost his luggage, trying in vain to communicate in a language he barely understands. Instead, I made the situation worse.

I spotted a woman in a bright orange vest, clipboard in hand, on the far side of the baggage carousel, and I decided that she was my best bet. I readied myself with the best Chinese I could muster and told her plainly that I could not find my luggage. She seemed astonished to hear me pipe up in Mandarin.

"You speak Chinese?" she asked, her mouth agape. I was sure that she hadn't even registered my question.

"Yes," I said. "I can speak a little." I pinched two fingers together as if to give the amount a physical quantity. Then, as if still reeling from her first victory of being understood, she said something quickly that I did not understand, and she sighed, beckoning me to follow her down the hall.

She sat me down in a badly ventilated gray hull of a room to exchange pleasantries with a couple of the other airport attendants as she went to investigate the issue. I sat nervously and smiled, as the staff split their attention between me and the soccer match that was coming in over the weathered color display. They asked me questions like where I was from and why I had come to China. I told them that I had flown in from New York and their eyes widened. "The Big Apple," they said in unison, as if it were the most natural response. I said that I got a job in China, that I would be an English teacher in Taigu. Before long, other airline officials started showing up, almost always preceded by a smile or a giggle, as if only to catch a glimpse of the delusional foreigner who claimed to be living in China's backwaters for the next two years.

To my credit, I wasn't entirely oblivious about the town before I arrived. Taigu had been described in the Shansi handbook as lying in the heart of Shanxi province, about an hour away from the capital city of Taiyuan and seven hours southwest of Beijing in the north of China. The county was home to roughly 50,000 people, which to an outsider might sound like a lot, but by Chinese standards was remarkably small. As a largely agricultural village, most people were farmers, and much of the land was studded with large swaths of fields for tilling. Near the center of town, there was an old section with cobbled streets and traditional architecture that scarcely still existed elsewhere in China.

A part of me found it endearing just how curious people were of me; I gathered from their expressions that foreigners didn't fly to Taiyuan all that often. At the same time, I began to feel embarrassed about how many thoughts I had and how few of them I could actually express. I tried to focus on the soccer game so I wouldn't have to answer any more questions. Finally, the woman in the orange vest returned. She told me that my bags were still in Beijing and that it was already too late to get them but that they would be delivered to the post office in Taigu first thing the following morning. Again, a confused look spread across my face. She guided me to the area just past the baggage claim where Li Feng was one of just a handful of people still left pacing back and forth.

Li Feng shook my hand and flashed a tight smile. He was a short man and not particularly imposing. He had a slender figure and wore a pair of horn-rimmed glasses that made his eyes look searching and nervous. Almost immediately he started in with the airline attendant. I couldn't tell what they were talking about, but there was a wry harshness to his voice. It surprised me how aggressive the language sounded, how confrontational. After he was done, he related in English what the attendant had said—and that I didn't have to worry about my bags. I tried to apologize about how long I had made him wait, but he just waved me off.

"This is my job," he said. There was a quiet resignation to his tone. Outside of the airport, it was raining hard. Li Feng pulled out a big umbrella for the two of us to share, and I held my single carry-on close to my chest as we waded through the parking lot.

"Does it rain like this here a lot?" I asked him, almost shouting, as the rain swallowed the end of my sentence. He squinted at me.

"Only when we're picking up foreigners."

He led me to the car, and the driver took us to a restaurant not far from the airport for dinner. Li Feng told me that Nate, one of the second-year teachers at the university, would be arriving in from Shanghai later that night, so we would have dinner nearby and then go back to the airport to pick him up. The place looked like your typical family restaurant: a gaggle of friendly women to greet us at the door and some older gentlemen working the stoves in the back. When we came in, there were a couple of teenage boys and girls zipping around the room trying to find buckets to catch water leaking from the roof. The rain had tripped the electrical wires so they were running on back-up power from a generator. As a result, the dining area was only partially lit, like the three of us had been set up on a blind date.

The food was nothing like how I imagined Chinese food to be. The three of us shared four dishes—wood ear mushroom, cabbage in white sauce, soft tofu, and Kung Pao Chicken, a presumed favorite for newly-arrived foreigners. The chicken was minced into tiny pieces and stir-fried with chili peppers and diced carrots. They were not at all like the sweet, breaded permutations I was used to in the states. The plates were all arranged in the center of the table and we all took turns jabbing and poking at them with our chopsticks. I wondered why Americans didn't eat the same way, getting to try three or four dishes at every meal instead of one.

"You'll have to get used to using these," Li Feng said, holding up the chopsticks in his hand and laughing. The driver laughed and I did too, still scraping at the mushroom on my plate. I didn't have the heart to tell him that my mom was Chinese and that I grew up using chopsticks more than I did a knife and fork at home.

Because the driver didn't speak a word of English and I was still too nervous to really try out my Mandarin, conversation was directed almost solely through Li Feng. I peered up from my place setting periodically at the two of them, their chopsticks going directly from the dishes to their lips, never once landing in their own bowls. One of the waiters brought over to our table a stout bottle of clear liquid with only one character on the label that I could read—alcohol.

"You'll have to get used to this too," Li Feng chimed in, his mood already getting lighter. The driver again let out a deep laugh as Li Feng poured three shot glasses full of *baijiu*, the caustic fire liquor that I would come to know well. We followed the first shot up with a second. I was too drunk on courtesy to refuse. Each wave of the cheap, glorified rubbing alcohol felt like a religious awakening—a renunciation of everything that came before and a quixotic avowal to never drink again.

Partway through the meal, I needed to use the bathroom and I asked Li Feng to help me flag down a waiter. In China, I learned that wait staff don't check in on you during the meal, but shouting "waiter" in a crowded restaurant at the top of your lungs is not seen as impolite. The waitress—so jubilant to greet me that she was actually bouncing—led me out the front entrance of the restaurant, and, ducking under tree boughs, looped around to the back where she unlocked the door to a lopsided wooden hut.

"Bathroom," she said, in forced English, pointing inside. The rain was still coming down in sheets, and, with only a newspaper as cover, she swiftly disappeared back around to the front.

I like to think that sooner or later, everyone has *the* moment, where your brain retraces all of the steps that unfolded in order to arrive at a particular place. For me, standing in front of the outhouse in my first hour in China was that moment. I opened the door and stepped inside. The corrugated tin roof leaked. There was no light of any kind, so I relied on my American cell phone still wedged in my pocket to navigate. The toilet was no more than a hole that shot down four or five meters into the ground, already teeming with scraps of paper, maggots, and other debris. I treaded cautiously, trying hard to distinguish mud from shit, and held the two opposing walls as I lowered myself to squat.

When I returned from the outhouse back into the restaurant, Li Feng was paying the bill and I quickly gathered my belongings to leave. Back into the car, we were about to double back to the airport when Li Feng got a call from Nate. I was sitting in the backseat and could only hear bits and pieces of the conversation, but I knew that, whatever it was, it wasn't English. The two of them went back and forth in Mandarin, and Li Feng was more animated than I had seen him the entire evening. I thought about how fluid it sounded—how effortless—and how much I secretly envied Nate before I had even met him. I remembered my conversation with the airport attendants in Taigu. They asked why I came to China. *I got a job in China,* I told them. *I will be an English teacher.* Even if there was more to say, it was too soon to be able to communicate it.

Li Feng got off the phone and told me that Nate's flight had been delayed for at least another couple hours because of the rain, so we would head home and Nate would find his way back to Taigu on his own in the morning. The car ride was 40 minutes of bumps and sudden breaks along the beaten country road, but I still managed to fall asleep. When finally it was time to wake up, I opened my eyes to a long narrow road with trees lining either side of it.

I got out of the car and rubbed my eyes. I recognized the campus from photographs, but it was still too dark to make out anything specific. The driver waited by the car as Li Feng took me through a clearing in the trees and across a stretch of pavement that was either dirt, gravel, cement, or some bizarre combination of all three. Finally we stopped in front of a brick house with two large windows. Li Feng began fishing around in his pockets. I pulled the drawstring light at the left side of the door and the sky came alive with moths.

"This is for you," he said, handing me the key. "Just don't lose it." He waved me goodnight and turned to head down the crooked path back to the car. I watched him go just long enough to see his shadow fade against the trees.

I looked up at the light bulb and then down again at the mud tracks on my shoes. It had stopped raining and everything was shrouded in a dense mist. I reached out and shook the leaves on the date tree that hung just beyond the porch. There seemed to be this perfect stillness that I wanted to hold onto for as long as I could, this utter sense of calm. Nearby, storm waters were rising, and I knew the feeling wouldn't last.

GETTING MY FEET WET

In my first two weeks in Taigu, it rained nearly every day. Embankments were flooded and dirt and gravel roads bubbled over with mud. In the commercial area of campus where street vendors perennially sold food, bricks were laid in the street to form a walking path, and people clustered under the shelter of umbrellas and small awnings. It was odd weather given the location. China's north was known for its dryness—the stale dust that hung in the air and coated the inside of your mouth. Taigu's location low in a valley meant that rain traveling from the west often got dumped on mountain passes in Shaanxi or Inner Mongolia before it ever reached Taigu.

By most accounts, though, it was a nice change. Aside from the grayness, the rain brought a certain freshness to the day, replacing the sticky warmth with damp cool. We used to judge air quality by standing at the big track and informally gauging the clarity of the mountains way off in the distance—partly obscured was pretty good, and if we could make out any more than the general outline, it meant that it was a good day for running. On most days, though, it was just a slushy gray blur—an inkblot on the horizon—done up in water paint by some ancient Chinese calligrapher. If I hadn't known any better, I would have scarcely thought they were real.

It was hard to characterize those first days. Quite unlike my semester-long stay in Japan, coming to China was not accompanied by the incredible culture shock that I had anticipated. I chalked a lot of that up to my upbringing. However different rural China was from anything I'd ever experienced before, I felt an intrinsic connection to the place. The people, the places, the food, the sounds, even the smells, conjured a familiarity borne from the spiritual more than anything else. I was reminded of home-cooked dinners with my extended family, of walking through Flushing's Chinatown in the pouring rain, of makeshift squash gardens in the front yard, and of laundry hanging from the windows of tenement apartments. The faces I saw were simultaneously familiar and strange; they were coated with stories—of grief, wonder, hope, and sadness—some of which I already knew by heart.

For most of my first semester, I spent a lot of time with the other foreigners, who, like me, taught English at the university. My housemate Grant and I went through teacher training together in January, so we had already established a cursory acquaintanceship. He was twenty-four, had graduated college in 2007, and worked as a stonemason for two years in the Berkshires before coming to China. Nate and Rachel lived at house number thirteen, the brick and mortar flat located right next to ours. Both were twenty-three, East Asian Studies and English majors respectively, and had studied Mandarin for four years.

The four of us had graduated from Oberlin and had all been recipients of the Shansi Fellowship to get to China. The Fellowship was staggered so that Nate and Rachel were beginning their second years while Grant and I were starting our first. But there were two other American teachers who had more or less come on their own and were also in their first years. Darren graduated the same year as I did—making the two of us the youngest foreigners there. He had grown up on the outdoors—he loved snowboarding and camping—and I struggled initially to place him in Taigu where both of those things seemed inconceivable. Jerry arrived a little later than the rest of us. He was twenty-six, Korean-American, and had previously worked as a wedding photographer in Austin. He had always been interested in language and Mandarin, he said, and what better way to explore that than in China's rural countryside.

Aside from the six Americans, there was also an older German named Luca. It was his second year at the university teaching German to very wealthy third-tier Chinese students with pipe-dream aspirations of passing the German college entrance exam. On the surface, Luca was a 36-year-old alcoholic trying in vain to prolong his youth. We speculated the reasons why he came to China to teach—some falling out with either his family or his work that made him emigrate. All he told us was that by German standards he was poor and couldn't afford to go home. In China, he was treated like a king—as a teacher, his students' parents were forced to buy him everything when he visited their hometowns—put him up in four-star hotels, deliver imported beer to his door, and take him out to luxurious dinners at McDonald's.

When he was sober, it was a like a switch had been flipped, and he went from garrulous to silent, his humor resigned to discontent. On those rare occasions, we sometimes got him to speak about his sister and his homeland, both of which he missed dearly. But when he drank, his tone turned bitter. He hated a lot of the food in Taigu—not to mention the beer. And the same things that I would soon loathe—feelings of isolation, dirty surroundings, air that tasted of coal—also aggravated him. He smiled wryly when he explained that, illiterate and not conversational in Mandarin, he was the most ignorant man in all of China. In Germany as an intellectual, he was miserable—there were too many problems that he was made constantly aware of. But in China, bureaucracy scarcely bothered him because he didn't understand it.

We foreigners were regarded as enigmas—endlessly fascinating and mysterious. We were tall and big and ignorant and Western, but every once in a while, we could pass as Chinese. Occasionally there were no stares. Drivers didn't slow to gawk, street vendors didn't pause and look up from their cooking, young kids didn't point and giggle, and old people didn't take a second glance. Despite our small numbers, we comprised a motley crew whenever we went out to meals or walked around campus together.

For the first time in a long time, I found myself with very little to do and a lot of time in which to do it. The internet wasn't working, and I had already arranged and re-arranged my room countless times. I started watching some Chinese television with the hopes that comprehension would filter into my mind through osmosis, and did my best to do some character studying for a couple of hours every day. All of the other foreigners save for Jerry had had at least six months of in-country China experience already, so I came in with a considerable distance to make up.

Having arrived with only a year-and-a-half of formal study under my belt, it was hard to wrap my mind around a lot about the place: the nuances in the Shanxi dialect, how fast people spoke, and how staggeringly little I was able to understand at the outset. It would take some time before disparate, seemingly disjointed characters would come to shape comprehensible menu items, and I would actually be able to communicate with the handful of Chinese friends that we all inherited from Nate and Rachel.

In the unstructured free time that constituted the majority of those days, a lot revolved around simply talking and eating. At noon, the campus loudspeaker began piping out melodic Communist-era work songs to alert us all that it was time for lunch. Rui Wan, the cook hired by the Foreign Affairs Office, served lunch for the seven of us on weekdays in a one-room mess hall not far from our houses. The food was simple but good—a bowl of rice or noodles and a selection of stir-fried greens, some kind of meat dish, and, once a week, a brimming plate of home-made dumplings. On one of those first meals, I asked Rachel and Nate how they adapted to life here.

"So, what do you do for fun?"

"The same things you might do in the states," Nate respondidly placidly. "Drinking, eating, talking." He cleaned the end of the chopstick with his lips. "Only except here there are no bars or clubs and nothing's open past eleven." It made sense, considering that Taigu was such a small town that it had no mention in Lonely Planet, did not appear on Google Maps, and was over an hour away from the nearest Western fast food.

"Activities are pretty tame by traditional standards," he said with a grin. "That's why most of the fun we have to make ourselves."

Lunch was punctuated on either end by two-hour teaching periods in the morning and the afternoon. Immediately following, there was exercise: everything from running to swimming to playing basketball. At 6:30, we had dinner—usually out at one of the local restaurants on campus—and then it was back home for more lesson-planning, writing, and hanging out. Twice a week I had Chinese lessons with my tutor Leslie.

Many of the restaurants where we ate were located in North Yard. The campus of Shanxi Agricultural University was divided into two halves—North Yard and South Yard. Where North Yard was home to faculty housing, the vegetable market, an elementary school, and a host of small shops and restaurants where we took our meals, South Yard comprised the meat of the campus—replete with student dormitories, athletic fields, showers, cafeterias, administrative offices, classrooms, and our own living quarters.

At first glance, North Yard looked just like a big open-air market. Vendors were sandwiched side-by-side along both sides of the narrow sidewalk. Cars, bicyclists, and pedestrians all shared the middle roadway. There was almost every kind of street food imaginable—small hand-sized *bing* (pancakes) of all varieties, bubble tea, barbecued meat on skewers, fried tofu, vinegar-stained noodles, and fresh dates, for which Taigu was famous. At dinner each night, we lingered long after the food was finished. We often ate as a flock of foreigners punctuated with a few Chinese friends; rarely was conversation ever in one language.

Almost all of the food was exceptionally cheap—dabbling at a few such stands only ran between 50 cents and a dollar U.S., if that. On either side of the vendors, there were little stationary stores, delis, hair salons, and sit-down restaurants—far too large a selection, we gathered, to exhaust over two years even if we went to a new one for every meal. Dishes were all served family-style in the middle of the table in the order in which they were made. There was no tax or tip, and we usually took turns simply paying for the entire meal rather than splitting the check. We used sheets of toilet paper instead of napkins and drank boiled water with our food. Survival depended on your skill with chopsticks; without talent, one would surely starve in a group meal setting.

Once or twice a week, we splurged and went out to bigger meals that usually encompassed a wider circle—mostly Nate or Rachel's former students. For those bigger dinners, Rachel and Nate took us to some of their favorite restaurants in town. Despite its roughness around the edges, Taigu had a charming sleepy town feel—old women playing cards in the afternoon, tiny storefronts that doubled as family residences, small crowds of working folks who gathered after quitting time to chat. At the main intersection, there was still the glow of the single traffic light that acted as arbiter for the entire town.

Though there were always a few varieties to choose from, hot pot was a perennial favorite. At the center of the table was a large, boiling hot pot, and on the floor to its side was a small shelf full of raw ingredients that were added to the pot in stages—beginning with thin sheets of lamb, followed by the vegetables and ending with the wide, translucent noodles known as *fentiao*. The pot, wrought in the shape of a yin-yang symbol, divided the broth into clear and spicy.

Of the people we ate with, we tended to be divided pretty equally—and split along the length of the table accordingly. My roommate Grant and I always sat on opposite ends—he didn't care much for the clear broth at all, but the spicy one, blanketed in oily redness and pockmarked with kernels of black peppercorn, was something he never tired of. It felt a bit like fishing, to reel back the chopsticks and cast a line deep into the pot, revealing at passes a crab leg, a head of baby bok choy, or a cut of sweet potato.

Grant did a lot of the talking at meals, aided generously by a male cohort who were interested in many of the same topics.

"At what age does playing video games become a guilty admission rather than a point of pride?" he asked, just as the lamb was done and we were getting started on the vegetables.

"Never," Jerry and Nate both answered a bit too quickly.

"Video games are transcendent," Jerry continued. "Like literature or movies. They really shouldn't get the stigma they do in our culture."

Grant, who played video games himself, enjoyed being an agitator, but didn't like to lose an argument.

"But suppose you're thirty-five, you're not married, and you don't have a job—"

"You get addicted to porn and start feeling better about your life," Nate snapped back.

"Maybe that really graphic porn too, where the guy's foreskin tears from the impact," Darren replied with a sneer.

"In China, there is no porn," Luca piped up, a few beers deep. "Only massage." He made these terrible, squeezing motions with his hands. When conversation devolved, it did so spectacularly. Rachel, attempting to stay as far removed as she could, quietly doused each mushroom cap in a bowl of peanut sauce and washed the entire mixture down with a glass of boiled water.

For those first couple of weeks, I tried to really concentrate on lesson planning. I found myself rifling through Brian's—my predecessor's—old teaching binder, burying my head in textbooks still left behind on the bookshelf, and cycling through a half-dozen ESL teaching tool websites, searching for the perfect lesson. My goal was to have a certain chronology to my lessons, to scheme big picture themes instead of haphazardly stringing unrelated topics together. We each had our own strategy to teaching. While most of the first-year teachers were in the same boat, Nate made it no secret that he liked to wing his lessons, drawing on material from his first year and whatever else popped into his head in the morning before his first class.

Rachel and I did a lot of our lesson planning together—a fact that didn't go unnoticed by the other teachers. It probably didn't help that we did lots of other things together too—writing, painting, cooking. On the rare days when we could see the mountains beyond the big track, I went running with her off-campus, past the crop fields where farmers toiled until sundown, and into the back roads of neighboring towns and villages. Sometimes, we just read poetry and short stories together over mugs of peppermint tea. I could tell all the male energy really got to her at times. It was difficult for Rachel being the only foreign female in Taigu.

On Wednesdays, Luca had us all over for German Night, which basically just entailed all of us going to his house after dinner, eating imported German food, talking with Chinese students, and drinking lots of beer. It may not have sounded like much, but it was actually a nice way to break up the monotony of the workweek. Night life in Taigu revolved principally around the presence of alcohol. Beer was ordered at almost every dinner and tended to dictate a large portion of our weekend activities. It was true what Nate said: "When you live in the middle of nowhere, you have to find a way to occupy your time."

It made it even easier that we all lived so close to one another. The houses where we resided in pairs—Grant and I, Nate and Rachel, Darren and Jerry, and Luca (who lived alone)—could practically be drawn in a straight line, with no more than 100 meters separating any one of them from another. The trouble was that university students didn't live much further away than that either. They lived in these behemoth Pepto-Bismol-hued cinder-block towers located near the small track on the south side of campus. They were each about six stories high, and sometimes five or six of them would be spread out in a line, indistinguishable save for die-cast numbers etched into their sides.

I struggled initially with trying to find a balance between my life as a teacher and that of a peer. There was no privacy, and students from all across campus came over to the house to petition for "friendship," which was often just a front for payment-free English lessons. As foreigners, we were used to being daily spectacles. The unfortunate downside, though, was that most of the attention we got was unwanted, leaving us powerless to stop it without coming off as jerks. The students were all around my age and it was hard to be a distanced authority figure when part of the natural inclination of human beings is to want to make friends and connections in unfamiliar places.

Still, every Wednesday students and teachers alike converged on Luca's living room sofas. Like our own flats, Luca had his own bedroom, kitchen and bathroom, but because he didn't have a roommate, he had the living room all to himself. Compared to most amenities afforded to students at the school, our houses were remarkably nice. One reason why students were inclined to seek us out, I reasoned, was because our living rooms were much more conducive to holding conversation than staking out standing room in a crowded dorm that saw six students to every room.

It was usually at these outside functions that I got the majority of the questions. As a mixed-race Chinese, there was a whole other level to my experience living there that lay beneath the surface. Some took my foreignness at face value. But others took the time to ponder. They wondered why my hair was black and my eyes were dark, and they started to form the same question in their minds: "Why do you look like me?" I struggled each time to find the right answer. But still they smiled back, politely, as if all of life could be explained so simply.

SETTLING IN

After a while, confusion may begin to set in. You may become impatient with making simple mistakes. Mundane tasks like mailing a letter seem to take forever and leave you exhausted. Comparisons with previous Shansi Fellows will undoubtedly be made and this may begin to bother you. You will probably also begin to have some trouble with your stomach.

Some weekend side trips may begin to look tempting. They may seem to provide evidence of progress. "I learn so much more in a day of traveling than in a day of work at the campus." You may be in search of the same kind of exhilaration you had when you first arrived. It may be important to resist this temptation and concentrate instead on understanding your immediate surroundings. This takes time and lots of grubby work. You may also have run yourself down physically and emotionally now to the point where you begin to wonder if you are an invalid. You should now take stock and restore your energies.

CLIMBING THAT OTHER GREAT WALL

Not yet one full week into my two-year commitment in Taigu, and I was ready to leave. Maybe the rain was starting to get to me, or the air, or the overwhelming feeling of being an outsider. The days that lingered on did so without respite, and I didn't want to burden my Senior Fellows with the grief and trouble of entertaining me when there was nothing for me to do. I figured that learning to cope with bouts of boredom and loneliness were all part of the necessary culture-shock experience, but already my patience was beginning to wear thin. I was thankful in some ways for the solitude, but at the same time I was anxious for classes to start and for life to really begin.

Without many other options, I tried my hand at simply living in the present. Rachel helped by introducing me to two of her good friends—Bobby and Lynn. It was an off-year, she told me. Friendships in Taigu worked in cycles, and every two years there was a turnover, the same way it was with the foreigners. It always took the first year or two to get to know someone, and by the time you really put roots down, it was time for one or both of you to leave. Many of the friends Rachel made over her first year had graduated and Bobby and Lynn were two of her only former students who she was still close to.

Lynn was full of an exuberance almost unseen at the university. There wasn't an apathetic bone in her body; her thirst for new experiences was almost exhausting. She took even the most banal excuse to leave campus—a visit to the pet shop to buy cat food—and spoke English better than any Chinese person I would meet in Taigu. Bobby was a sarcastic wisecrack who exuded a kind of nerdy cool. He was a treasure trove of knowledge on internet memes and online gaming. They were together so often that they could have practically been siblings. Both wore thick glasses and dressed in the range of mangled English-language t-shirts and generic-looking blue jeans that I would come to expect from my own students. I was amazed at how close Rachel and the two of them were with each other, like they had known each other all their lives.

I met them both on my second day in Taigu. It was Lynn's birthday and Rachel insisted that we all go out into town to celebrate. Slightly jet-lagged but desperate for an amicable first impression, I agreed. The four of us—Bobby, Lynn, Rachel and I—walked to one of the big KTV—karaoke—halls in town. Almost all of the buildings had an aged quality to them—some in an antique, gilded sort-of elegance, and others simply because they were falling apart and covered in dirt. The land that wasn't left for tillage was wrapped up in crumbling old-style pagodas interspersed with hastily-built concrete high-rises, all laid within a dirt and gravel road system that was constantly being paved and re-paved.

I found it weird, just the four of us sitting around a spacious parlor booth and singing songs into a giant feedback machine at four in the afternoon, but I was the outsider and the one who needed to adapt to my new surroundings. At Bobby's urging, Rachel and I exhausted the handful of palatable English songs available, going so far as to croon "My Heart Will Go On" with tone-deaf fervor. After a couple hours, the cake arrived, and no sooner was I trying to sample a bite when Bobby and Rachel both attacked Lynn's face with icing.

"It's a tradition," Lynn said begrudgingly. "Good luck for the birthday girl." It was fitting that the cake wasn't really made for consumption, I thought, given that it tasted like building insulation.

Since it was getting dark, we decided to take a cab back to campus. They sat me in the front seat next to the driver, and the three of them did the talking from the back. The asphalt pavement had long been sheared off the road, and cars and motorcycles were darting around the exposed holes and mounds of earth that were placed haphazardly in the street like landmines. Our cab was zipping by as three lanes of traffic merged into one and then just as quickly fanned back out to three. I had never experienced anything like it.

"Did you see that?" I asked Rachel.

"What?"

"The way he's driving," I said astonished, "I feel like I'm going to die." Bobby and Lynn couldn't stop laughing.

"Welcome to China," Rachel said as she gingerly counted out the money for the fare.

A few days later, Rachel announced that she would be going to Beijing to visit some friends for the weekend and invited me to come. I jumped at the opportunity. Unlike all of the other Fellows, I hadn't spent any time in the capital city. Aside from the three-hour layover in Beijing, my first and only impression of China was of its countryside. Though Taigu was bearing down on me, I was nervous about the trip; I felt like I had barely settled in and feared that even a short trip away would cause the few roots I had put down to be wrenched from the ground.

Bobby was busy that weekend, but Rachel extended the invitation to Lynn, whose boyfriend lived in Beijing. Like me, Rachel was mixed-race, and thanks to family on her dad's side—her Chinese side—she had a handful of distant relatives who lived in China. Rachel told me that we could stay at her great aunt and uncle's apartment, avoiding the trouble of finding and paying for a hostel.

There was something about close female friends that was immensely comforting, and neither Rachel nor I connected incredibly well with the other foreign men in Taigu. But I also knew that the initial stages of friendship were delicate—that two people could grow tired of each other in the same span of time it took for them to be propelled towards one another in the first place. I recognized this and tried to preempt it by devising my own itinerary for the time that Rachel would be spending with friends, and reconciling myself with being alone.

Our journey began at 7:00 AM sharp—with just enough time for me to pack, change, and get to the train station headed first toward Taiyuan, and then by fast train to Beijing. We arrived in Taiyuan in time for breakfast—a short meal of *zhou*, rice porridge, this time sweetened with fruit. With a decent amount of time to kill, we decided to walk to a public park. Park culture, as I had learned from textbook readings from my elementary Chinese class at Oberlin, was very big in China. Most parks were free, but the well-known ones cost a bit of money to enter. The one we chanced upon featured a small amusement park—a miniature Coney Island, complete with a tiny rollercoaster, merry-go-round, and a few carnival games sprinkled amidst food vendors and other stands.

When I shared with Lynn what I remembered from the textbook—that visiting Chinese parks was a great way to observe the daily life and customs of Chinese people—she just shook her head and laughed.

"No one goes to parks to observe natural life," she told me in English. "People go there to live their own lives, separate from others, and in that way, they can enjoy one another's company harmoniously." The Chinese government loved that word—harmonious—and it was used on so many slogans and billboards that it quickly became two of the characters I recognized most.

The three-hour trip to Beijing was wrought with small conversation and shut-eye. Rachel was situated between Lynn and me. The two of them chatted eagerly back and forth while I slept fitfully against the window. Since Rachel spoke Mandarin well, they talked mostly in Chinese. I couldn't follow it, so every time I woke up, I just stared out at the window, watching the scenery change. There were incredible terraced fields carved out of the mountains filled with plants and small trees. Space was at a premium; every square inch was mined for its optimal economic capacity.

With her head turned to face Lynn, I stole glances at Rachel from time to time. I admired the way her ponytail bounced every time she laughed and noted how her chest heaved up and down with every jerk of the train. She had been my closest confidante since coming to Taigu, but it was more than that. She was an incredible source of knowledge about everything. I looked up to her. She took to calling me *di di*, "little brother," which I found endearing until I discovered that I was attracted to her. Lynn was the closest friend Rachel had in Taigu and I wanted to respect that— but at the same time, I realized that without a grasp of the language or the city, I would be dependent on her to get around.

When we arrived in Beijing, we got on a bus and headed straight for Rachel's great aunt's apartment. The trip wasn't long, and before we knew it, we arrived at an aging, four-story tenement building in the center of the westernmost quadrant of Beijing. It looked like it could have been one of the rare apartments that had managed to stay intact through the Cultural Revolution, from the days when real estate around Beijing was still relatively cheap and before massive high-rise apartment complexes were built to replace smaller family homes. The stairs creaked and wailed and at each floor a light flickered on, detecting motion. At the top of the fourth flight, Rachel's great aunt and uncle emerged from a polished wooden door to meet us.

Her great uncle was clearly a bit older and feebler than her great aunt. He walked with a cane and his face was pockmarked with dark age spots that blemished his skin like craters. Her great aunt was animated and garrulous, and spoke feverishly with Rachel, the great niece she hadn't seen in months.

"You made it," she said in Mandarin, giving Rachel a tight squeeze on the shoulders. "And how were your summer travels?" She greeted Lynn and I summarily and urged us to put our bags down in the living room. She hung up the wide, red smock that she was wearing to clean around the house and ushered us out to dinner at a nearby restaurant.

Both the great aunt and uncle were regulars at the place. At the front entrance, a man with a suit and a headset radioed for three beautiful young waitresses, all dressed in traditional *qipao,* to help Rachel's great uncle climb up the stairs to the restaurant. We ordered perhaps more food than I had seen in my entire week in Taigu up to that point (and we were no eating slouches in Taigu, either), including some of the famed, oft-exalted Beijing *kaoya,* or roast duck. The food was incredible, and for the five of us—great aunt and uncle included—it was a feast. In typical Chinese fashion, we were urged to eat and drink mercilessly, this time, thankfully without the added ingestion of alcohol. Even still, by meal's end, and despite a litter of exhausted plates and stomachs, we ended up taking a few whole dishes to go.

As strange as it was, my disposition towards Rachel's relatives was almost viscerally familiar—one that had evolved after years of careful study of my own extended family. At the dinner table, each conversation began the same way: her great aunt posed a question, and I, as the dutiful and polite guest, was naturally expected to respond. Her husband, like older males in my mother's family, preferred reticence, but I could tell that she herself was excited. Here I was, another *part*-Chinese, her kind, the kind of person with whom she could joke and not worry about offending. She wore a face I knew well—beady eyes, a wide grin, and a nod to egg you on despite reservation. And almost reflexively, I was all but ready to deliver the culmination of my childhood knowledge of Cantonese—the perfected smile-and-nod routine— until I realized that I could understand her. Or, perhaps—more accurately—that I should have been able to.

That was because she was not speaking Cantonese, the bane of my childhood insecurities, but Mandarin, the very language I had been studying for over a year. Not only that, but she was speaking the most standardized regional dialect. And still, there was nothing. My head registered sounds but no meaning: a garble of tones and nonsensical word pairings. I managed to half-register a reply before sinking back down in my chair. For a time, a few short exchanges were all it took to shatter any hopes I had pinned on my study of Mandarin. It was such a debilitating feeling to have to disappoint someone, not for lack of effort, but out of sheer inability. As she began to realize my lack of understanding, I saw the familiar sag of the face, the smile drawn downwards, air blown out from between her lips. It was particularly hard that I looked like her; all the familiar marks of a Chinese but without the means to communicate.

I decided to ask Rachel about it.

"It's difficult for any American-born Chinese who can't speak their mother tongue," she told me. "Even for us halfies."

"So what did you do about it?"

"I got teased mercilessly." She gave another impassioned laugh. "Even after I started studying Mandarin, my relatives joked about my accent and the way I put sentences together." Chinese families are universally hard to please.

I nodded. "It's like spending your whole life being perceived one way and constantly underperforming those expectations." I thought about Jerry in Taigu and how people in the town couldn't understand why a Chinese-looking guy could only speak rudimentary Mandarin.

"It's not as bad as all that," Rachel said, touching me lightly on the shoulder. "It may take a while, but you'll figure it out."

I was perhaps luckier in that I didn't always *look* Chinese, at least to a lot of people in northern China. It was only when people noticed the color of my hair or the shape of my eyes that it seemed to register. Sometimes it was easier to pass simply as American—with no hopes latched onto my presumed knowledge of Chinese language, custom, and mannerism. In that way, no one got hurt.

After dinner, the five of us went back to Rachel's great aunt and uncle's apartment. When we were all seated around the living room, Rachel's great aunt brought out a tray of strange-looking pastries that she had baked for us to try for dessert. We were all so full that we could barely stand, but it was rude to refuse food, and so I picked up the thick flaky pastry and plopped it down on a paper plate on my lap. I was trying to discern what exactly it was, when finally, I had the courage to ask the great aunt.

"What is this," I asked, using the extent of my Mandarin. The great aunt leaned in and shook her head, playfully chiding me for my cultural ignorance.

"*Yue bing,*" she said, and looked over at Rachel for a translation.

"Mooncake," Rachel whispered between forced bites.

It was the end of September and all of China was gearing up for the yearly mid-autumn festival, for which mooncakes were the traditional food. Still, I was perplexed at just how these pastries came to pass as mooncakes. Mooncakes were the stuff of my own family gatherings—the sweet globules of chewy, rich goodness indicative of southern China. These northern mooncakes were wide and flat, stuffed with a filling of salty meat, seasoned and spiced, that tasted more like a quiche than a dessert. Before I came to China, I was scarcely aware of the country's polarity—not simply with regard to food, but also standard of living, climate, levels in education, and even how people looked.

The whole situation struck me as this oddly parallel universe. Rachel's relatives, like my own, spoke a language that I didn't understand—but this time a different dialect. They lived in an apartment, strikingly similar to that of my aunt in Queens—but in Beijing. I came to the conclusion that older Chinese people must actually share a similar lifestyle, in the same way that stereotypical older white suburbanites do. Trading in the sticky plastic coverings that overlie couches and the dingy, off-color draping, older Chinese couples might superimpose excessively large pieces of furniture in cramped quarters, and years' worth of boxed belongings, stacked floor-to-ceiling behind long pieces of fabric.

I was no stranger to that lifestyle. I remembered well the tiny outdoor porch where my aunt used to hang clothes and store bulky appliances, the living room that smelled of stale carpeting and moth balls, and her kids' bedrooms, which, after long years without use, had become part-time capsule and part-storage closet. Like the endless stretch of terraced fields on the way from Taiyuan, I remembered how every inch of space was monopolized, and the way each saved item functioned like a comforting reminder of the past. Living through the Cultural Revolution seemed to make Chinese perpetual pack rats in the same way it did for Americans who were alive during the Great Depression.

For the duration of the trip, Rachel slept in the adjoining guest room to her great aunt, and I slept in the great uncle's study atop a covered mattress in a far corner of the room. While there, I was guilty of a little snooping. Sure enough, there was something of the familiar—her great uncle's study had tables and bookshelves bursting with old magazines, newspaper clippings, and expired advertisements. There, too, were the same antique lamps, the coarse wool blankets slumped over the bed and chair, and the crinkly old wallpaper that hung ominously like a too-big coat. We wore slippers inside, ate communally at a makeshift dinner table in the living room, and always tried to look busy.

On my first night, the three of us went out after dinner to stock up on snack supplies and water. The next day, we would all be climbing a section of the Great Wall together with a couple of Rachel's friends who were also in Beijing for the first time. The whole time to and from the convenience store, Rachel and Lynn were giggling and talking in this fast, syncopated Mandarin that I could barely register. As my eyes glanced over the packaged cookies and dried fruits, I felt like they had abandoned me; that I was this intruder disturbing the harmony of their friendship, and that in some ways, I shouldn't have been there at all. I was jealous of their closeness, of a kind of relationship that I wanted so badly for myself.

Sleep was in short supply as all three of us were out of bed well before 5:30 in the morning and on a taxi on our way to the youth hostel where Rachel's friend Kate and her boyfriend Tom were staying on the other side of Beijing. We were lucky that their hostel had trips running out to the Great Wall on a nearly daily basis and we just happened to pick a good day to join up with them. The whole package was a little pricey, but it included all of the necessary admission tickets for the wall (they charge you at junctures spaced somewhat arbitrarily throughout) and the round-trip bus ride, which took just about three hours each way.

Not knowing the specifics of the Beijing itinerary before packing, I was somewhat at a loss for proper hiking attire. More than that, I figured a weekend rendezvous in posh Beijing would be the perfect place to break in the new shoes I had bought just one day before leaving the states, and which I had yet to try on.

Shoes aside, the trek was great. We went from Jinshanling to Simatai, a stretch of over 30 watchtowers that took about four hours to traverse. It was hard not to marvel at the incredible scale and majesty of it all. The walk was gratifying and exhausting, taking in the climbs and descents that characterized each tower. Nearing the end of our hike, there were quite a few sections of the Wall that were being outfitted with new bricks and cement as a result of erosion. *There are cracks in every wall's defense,* I reasoned. *It is just a matter of knowing how to conceal them.*

Another three-hour bus ride and a quick dinner later, I got back to Rachel's great aunt and uncle's place that night feeling like my feet were on fire. Lynn had gone to sleep at her boyfriend's house and Rachel's relatives were already asleep. I kicked off my shoes, slid on a pair of slippers, and waited for my turn in the shower. Rachel had gone in first, and I was biding my time in the great uncle's study, coursing over the dusty negatives that were adhered with yellow-brown tape to the mirror.

I thought about the fading Polaroid stills and how tenuous our link to the past is—where it begins and how ultimately it falls to us to perpetuate and sustain. The Chinese relatives that I did have in China had completely lost contact with my family in the states—and perhaps the only place they still existed was in the handful of old images stowed away somewhere in shoeboxes.

Rachel came out of the shower in a towel looped around her midsection and chest. Her hair was still wet and cascading over her shoulders. I caught myself staring hard at her before turning away and sheepishly gathering up my belongings. There was this casual beauty about her and the way she carried herself as she made her way through the cramped living room.

"Goodnight," she said. "You're going to feel so good after that shower."

I laughed. "I don't know, I feel pretty good now," I said, my mouth moving faster than my brain could process. She cocked her head and raised her left eyebrow. "Goodnight," I said, trying hard to cover my tracks, and wrapped my arms awkwardly around her.

She pulled back a bit from the hug before retreating to her room. Silently cursing myself, I quickly shuffled into the bathroom and locked the door behind me.

It was only then that I began to understand some of the differences between this apartment and my aunt's apartment in Queens. Principal among them was the fact that my relatives enjoyed some of the comforts of a Western lifestyle that had not spread to the vast majority of China's population. And so, even despite knowing this, it still managed to shock me that instead of a traditional Western shower, I found myself standing in a bathtub almost comically small for my size, holding a bucket of lukewarm water in one hand and a fussy showerhead in the other.

In that instant, the comforts of American hygiene fell away. I was laughing at myself, squinting through the screen of an open window and hoping that no one could see me wielding two instruments I scarcely thought could work in tandem. The showerhead alternated blasts of scalding hot water into the shallow bucket, and I squatted down, slowly pouring it over my hair and body. The pipes clanged and gargled and I feared for a moment that this—my—shower would be the aging apartment's last. I managed to hose myself down without making too much of a mess, and with no excess of grace, hoisted myself out of the tub and back to the great uncle's study, where I slept as soundly as I could have hoped—all things considered.

TEACHING
CLASS
AND
TAKING
NAMES

I woke up in a cold sweat on the morning of my first class. It was so dark that I could scarcely make out the outline of my room, but my body was convinced that I was late. I lay transfixed in bed, certain of my aberration but too scared to confirm it. Images filled my head: a classroom swelling with students, the vacant podium where a teacher ought to be standing, bells signaling the start of class, the methodical pulse of a clock's second hand.

Slowly, I pulled myself out of bed, and with a weary eye, confronted the time. 5:17 AM—still over two hours until class. I let out a long breath, tiptoed back to bed, and lay there, trying to go back to sleep. As anticipated, my alarm sounded just over an hour later, but I was still awake. My mind was consumed with worst-case scenarios: *What if my lesson is too boring? What if my students can't understand me? How will their perception of me affect their attitude towards Americans—towards foreigners in general?*

I had spent the better part of two days fiendishly hacking away at my first lesson—working it over with Rachel in her living room.

"I'll start with introductions," I said, "Then go straight into ground rules and expectations for the class." I had decided that the crux of my grading rubric would be based on attendance and participation, with homework and the final skit rounding out the rest. Rachel nodded at me, cross-referencing the lesson plan she had cobbled together for her first year.

"And after that?" she asked, like an army sergeant at boot camp. "After that I'll give them their names, take their photos, and give them a chance to ask me any questions they want."

"Just be prepared for some weird ones," Rachel noted, before returning to the careful stack of student surveys she had photocopied and readied for class.

I did know a couple of things about the teaching situation beforehand— small tidbits I had gleaned from Rachel and Nate as well as our supervisor, Zhao Huang, who ran down our schedules and gave us a brief pep-talk in Chinese on Sunday about our classes. She was a wizened woman with all the strut and confidence of a mother hen. We were her nest of baby chicks gathered from halfway across the world; she didn't want to see any of us fail.

"Your students will be nervous about having a foreign teacher," she told us. "But so as long as you stay calm and don't stir the pot, you will do fine." Rachel translated some of the harder phrases into English for me. "Remember, the nail that sticks up gets hammered down." It sounded especially grave and ominous in my head.

Evidently her advice didn't catch on. During a ten-minute break during my very first class, some of my undergraduate students remarked that I looked so nervous I might be sick.

"Your hands are shaking," they cooed. "You should try to relax."

I realized that my nervousness stemmed less from speaking in front of a large group of people, than it did from letting people down who trusted me to do my job well. My students were counting on me to be a good teacher—to have credentials and to be able to adequately teach them—and it was my responsibility to follow through. Gone were the days when, feeling particularly unmotivated, I could have simply gone through the motions as a student. No longer was I a spectator or a sideshow contributor; I was the entire three-ring circus.

I taught four different Oral English classes, each with about thirty students. Three of them were graduate student classes that met twice a week. The fourth was a class of undergraduate English majors whom I saw once a week. Each class period was two hours long, and in all I ended up teaching seven classes totaling fourteen hours every week. Though the undergraduates were all college students, the dynamic felt a little bit like high school. I was only a couple of years their senior, but I often felt much older.

With my graduate students, I had the opposite problem. With no exception, they were all older than I was, most just a year or two, but some upwards of ten or more—the equivalent of "continuing education students" and teachers in other departments who were interested in studying English. It felt incredibly strange to be teaching students who were older than me, mostly because I couldn't understand why they kept coming back to class. After all, what could some American, fresh out of college, really teach them about anything? For most of them, I was the first foreign teacher they had ever had.

Shanxi Agricultural University was what could be referred to as a mid-tier school: it didn't require tremendously high scores on the college entrance examination, but it did rank higher than the private vocational colleges that accepted students who failed the test outright. As an agricultural university, most of the students came from working class backgrounds, their mothers and fathers farmers themselves. Their majors were all agriculture-related, but in subjects as wide-ranging as ecology, forest protection, landscape architecture, crop genetics, soil science, and veterinary medicine.

Whereas American education was by and large "student-centered," in China, lecturing and rote memorization were the primary tools at a teacher's disposal. Students were accustomed to being passive learners in traditional classes that involved little-to-no class participation. Professors assigned experiments and homework and expected students to spit back key terms and data for exams.

Though this is not unheard of in America, in my experience as a student, I found it to be more the exception than the rule. However, as teachers we now had the power to change that through a fair bit of flexibility, creativity, and patience. My hope was to eventually be able to scrap the "lecture model" of teaching and spend the majority of every class emphasizing small group work so that students could actually practice the language. Before I arrived, I thought it would simply be a matter of putting conversation topics on the board and having students pair off.

But it proved more difficult than that. No one was conditioned to learn in that way. Even starting class with a hearty *how are you?* netted blank stares. I didn't doubt that my students were smart, hard-working, and motivated to learn, and I was aware of the stereotype about book smarts afforded to Asian Americans in the states. Most students in China grow up in a culture that stresses very little real world experience outside of schooling, leading to our frustrations about lack of freethinking in the classroom. Students aren't motivated to learn because going to school is the sum-total of all they are habituated to do.

There were other challenges too. The first was the length of the class period. A two-hour class certainly felt unwieldy at times, even when simply trying to hold a class's attention. Often, it seemed more beneficial to have four one-hour classes per week instead. But we devised good ways to remedy that problem, taking a ten-minute break at around the one-hour mark, and letting our students out ten minutes early so that they could get to their next class on time.

The second challenge was the classrooms themselves. My English majors' classroom didn't have a board of any kind, but rather, a projector hooked up in quite elaborate fashion to a computer. Theoretically, this made it easier to use advanced technology when planning a lesson, but it ended up being more inconvenient than anything else. Thankfully, my graduate students' classroom had a blackboard, so when demonstrating how to spell a word or assigning discussion questions, my students didn't have to squint at a tiny palm-sized computer screen by their desks to read it. However, in both classrooms, the desks and chairs were bolted resolutely to the floor, with all of the attention directed forward at the teacher.

Another major challenge was assessing my students' language levels. Within any given class, there was a wide discrepancy in the level at which my students performed—while some seemed near fluent (at least conversationally), others could barely string together a complete sentence without asking for help from their classmates in Chinese. It also seemed that many, if not all, of my students could read and write at levels three and four times higher than they could speak. Trying to mitigate those wide inconsistencies proved difficult, and so oftentimes I ended up relying on those higher-level students to act as language shepherds for those who were struggling.

The final challenge was in designing lessons. Without a textbook or teaching materials of any kind, we were given almost total freedom to plan and implement a curriculum. Though it was incredibly nerve-racking to have to parse out individual topics and lessons from the sheer vastness of material out there, it also enabled us to be creative about having to pick and choose which aspects of English language and culture we were most passionate about teaching.

It helped immensely, though, that I had five other American teachers that I could work with and bounce ideas off of. And it also helped that the Chinese model of education seemed to build-in an immense amount of respect for educators—much more so than that in the states. To say that you were a teacher in China set you apart as a professional. In class, the students were incredibly courteous—they apologized profusely if they were late, volunteered to wipe the blackboard after class, and stopped talking immediately when you started speaking.

I had always been a big proponent of the "fake it 'til you make it" approach to doing something with which you are unfamiliar at first. Teaching, for me, was no different, but after a short time, I really began to believe in my role. This was no small discovery, as previous to this experience, I would never have pegged myself as an educator. I didn't think I had the confidence or the motivation necessary to pull it off. It felt empowering to dress up every morning in slacks, a blazer, and dress shoes, all with a messenger bag full of ready-to-impart knowledge slung over my shoulder. I felt like a kid trying on my dad's tie for the first time.

It wasn't long before my students smiled and waved when they saw me, and I left each class with the sticky soft sensation of chalk still clinging to my fingertips. Despite my request to simply be called Daniel (as the title of "professor" required a degree that I couldn't rightfully say I'd acquired), half of my students called me "teacher," and more than a handful staunchly resolved to call me "sir." I'd even developed some of the telltale traits of English teachers—learning how to speak *slowly*, enunciate my words, pace my sentences, and repeat phrases until they stuck.

I was still new to it all on the first day when I gave my students their English names. It was traditional for students to receive English names just as we had all been given Chinese names when we started learning the language. I likened my students to amorphous lumps of clay, who, despite having studied English for upwards of ten years, still lacked a certain primordial identity. Giving them names was a weird sort of christening into the English-speaking world. But it was for that very reason that I felt so panicked—I found myself seated with immense responsibility just minutes after meeting them. *How could I possibly uncover enough about a person in so short a time to decide what their English face to the world would be?*

Luckily for me, unlike in Chinese, most English names didn't come with an incredibly complex back story—though names were necessarily derived from different cultures, their meanings weren't intrinsically linked to the individual components that make them up. Names like "Chris" or "Barbara" weren't really all that different from "Thomas" or "Samantha" save for subjective preferences and the feelings we have associated with them from past experience.

Different teachers had varying approaches on how to give names. Whereas Nate mostly named his students after friends and American celebrities—with both Rihanna and Eminem in the same class—and Grant had his students choose from an exhaustive list of the 500 most common English names, I decided to take a more *laissez-faire* approach to name-choosing.

The results were certainly mixed. I got a fair share of the sports-related (James after Lebron James, Owen after Michael Owen), the famous (Bruce after Bruce Lee), and those influenced by popular culture (Nemo and Clark). Then, of course, there were the downright strange—Ripal, Era, Rainbow, and Marhone. One of my more inquiring students settled on the name Karl Marx, while his seatmate wrote down the name Hitler, gesturing to himself. I allowed Marx; Hitler was the only name I turned down.

A lesson on name-choosing in China: Candy is not a stripper name. Neither is Cherry, Angel, Lotus, Snow, or Sky. Spring is a boy's name, as is Breath, Caitlin, and Dandelion. Obama is a mild-mannered sophomore who sits in the back of the class and doodles on his homework. Salt, Water, Rock, and Sea, are not strictly elements of the natural world. Peach, evidently, is not pleasing to the ear, but Grape is pleasantly well-received.

Armed with their new English names, what amazed me was how differently each student reacted to my request to take their photo. Since it was the first criterion with which I could use to judge them, I figured that most students would want to make a good impression. But where some smiled brightly and struck a pose, just as many were shy, gawky, or merely devoid of life. One student politely refused to have his picture taken in conjunction with his name, sighting the generally unsavory connection between a picture of a student holding a name placard and the mug shots of hardened criminals from American movies he had seen. At his request, I allowed him to take his picture without it.

Next came the question-and-answer session where the topics felt more than a bit self-serving. For a while, the entire room was silent, but slowly, one-by-one, students began opening up. More often than not, the questions were not particularly beguiling—most revolved around my perceived differences between America and China, whether I liked the taste of Chinese food, some general details about my academic and personal background, where I'd traveled to in China and abroad, whether I'd adjusted to life at the university, and if I was able to eat with chopsticks.

But what never failed to go unasked in each of my classes—always at the very end, and after I'd already asked, twice, if there were no other questions—was whether or not I had a girlfriend. The first time I heard it, the query caught me off-guard and I stammered before saying that *no, I didn't*. My answer set off a barrage of stifled giggling and a cacophony of oohs from the boys in the class. There was something glamorous about being a halfie—making me just familiar and just foreign enough to be fawned over.

"See, you still have a chance," Allen exclaimed, nudging his seatmate Crystal gently in the shoulder.

Another student asked: "If there were only two girls left in the world—a Chinese girl and a Japanese girl—which one would you choose?" Again came a chorus of animated whispers and all of the students scooted up in their hard, unmoving chairs, waiting for my response. I knew the question was loaded. Chinese students tended to hold a negative opinion of their neighbors to the east—a well of resentment dating back to the Nanjing Massacre. Japan never apologized for the casualties inflicted upon the Chinese in the tumultuous lead-up to World War II, and now, over 70 years, later, it was still a flash point for contempt.

I thought about using it as a teaching moment—setting the tone right at the start that all people, no matter of what race or nationality, were worthy of respect. *This was why I came here,* I thought, *to challenge public opinion.* It was the same way I felt about the pro-democracy movement in Tiananmen Square, or about the contended sovereignty of Taiwan. Still, I remembered Zhao Huang's words at the meeting before class: *don't stir the pot, the nail that sticks up gets hammered down.* Maybe it wasn't so bad to play it safe. Nate warned me about one of the past foreign teachers at the school who taught a class on Tibetan independence and was never let back into the country.

"Both," I said to another round of gleeful intrigue. And then, knowing that even the most advanced students in the class wouldn't follow me, I added: "After all, I have to repopulate the Earth."

(KOREA)

THAT'S NOT ME

"The first thing you need to know about Koreans," he said, his body swerving to face me from the front seat of the cab, "is that we love to rank things." We were stopped at a stop light and he laughed. "See, I can't even help myself."

We were on our way to Eden, which was, as of that weekend, ranked the number one club in all of Seoul.

"The trouble is," Bart went on, "the rankings are changing constantly. Everyone wants to be number one, so they're having grand re-openings all the time to try and steal back the title."

There were four of us in the car: Bart, Paul, Paul's girlfriend Sari, and me. The three of them had all lived in Korea for a time, but Bart was the most senior among them with two years under his belt. He was working for the Seoul Tourism Board and it was part of his job to host guests from out of town, so my visit wasn't unusual. He knew the city well, and spent his weekends frequenting an astounding number of its bars and clubs. Most of the reason I went to Korea was to visit Paul, a good friend of mine from college. He went to Korea after graduation, while I went to China. Sari was his girlfriend of the past two months whom he met online and already was making plans to move in with back in the states.

We had already been driving for about ten minutes from Paul and Bart's shared apartment in central Seoul. It struck me as I looked around the cab that I was the least Asian among them: Paul and Bart were both fully Korean American and Sari's family was from Taiwan. After a year in Taigu where I stood out as one of the only non-white foreign teachers, it felt odd, somehow, that I was now the whitest one among them, the only non-Korean speaker, and the new scapegoat for when strangers asked us why we were going to Itaewon—the most notorious neighborhood for foreign tourists in Seoul. I sunk down in the backseat, suddenly embarrassed by my race.

"Oh, before we go," Bart quickly whipped back around in the seat, "I want to show you something."

"Is this about—" Paul started saying.

"Yep," Bart finished. "I want him to see Hooker Hill."

The cab stopped and Bart paid the fare, waving us off. "You guys got the one home," he said.

The cab pulled off in front of a foreboding uphill plain. Just a block away from a large, well-lit 7-11, the hill spread out before us in unabashed splendor. Bart lumbered in front of me—his tall, wide frame something of an anomaly for most Koreans and what probably gave him away as having grown up in America. Still, all told, he was quite handsome—with fine Korean features that some of my female students in Taigu would have gone crazy over. He gave me a run-down of the well-known landmarks like he was out doing one of his work tours.

"Here's Cancun," he said. "There was a stabbing there a couple of weeks ago; I wouldn't recommend going in. And oh, over there is King Club. I hear the girls are friendly but they'll charge you just for talking."

On either side were juice bars and boutiques all fronting as brothels. It reminded me of the neon-lit massage parlors and bathhouses, or of the "ladies of the three accompaniments"—drinking, dancing, and public groping, as they were known—who populated karaoke bars and teahouses in China.

Bart and I had been introduced to each other a few times in college. He was a year older than me, and though we hung out in similar circles, we never really got close. He had actually lived in Taigu for a year before I arrived—not through Shansi but on his own. Though we never overlapped in Taigu, I had heard a lot of stories about him—mostly of the drunken nights he spent with Nate and Luca, all of them in their first years. He and Nate would spend whole afternoons wandering around Taiyuan, going into arcades, eating foreign fast food. Rachel had told me about the casual relationship they had had—and how if not for Taigu she and Bart would have probably never had any reason to get together.

All along the strip, girls were literally bursting out of storefronts and onto the street. Every three or four steps, we came across another hostess bar with a velvety red curtain that opened up suggestively to reveal half-a-dozen of them dressed in their bras and panties, looking surprised and bashful—exposed to the chilly elements. It felt voyeuristic and disconcerting to see them done up like that, but I kept sneaking glances in spite of myself. It could have been make-up or clothing or seeing exposed skin for the first time in a long time, but it was mesmerizing. I found myself slowly tuning out what Bart was saying and finding it hard to pry my eyes away.

Perhaps sensing the sudden collective lack of interest, Bart pulled up alongside a boutique with huge glass doors that could have passed for the gates of Hell.

"Let's stop and get a drink," he said.

"Here?" Paul questioned, noting the ornate studded doorknobs and seedy air of a Clue murder mystery.

"No, I know an Irish pub a little ways up the hill. You've been there with me before. They have great drink specials on Tuesday."

Paul shook his head.

"No hookers there, trust me." Bart said.

"Wolfhound?" Sari asked. Bart nodded his head and we started again up the hill.

Once inside the bar, Bart ordered the first round of Jameson on the rocks—the special that night. Compared with Chinese *baijiu*, it was hard to call it a bargain, but in Korea, I knew better than to question it. The rest of the menu was pricey too, and though I was hungry, I decided it best not to buy anything to eat. It was rude not to order food at a Korean bar, I learned, but this was a Western place, and no one thought much of it. As it was, we would have had to order at least two different appetizers for the four of us so as not to look cheap. In Korea, most foods were ordered in pairs. There were other customs that Bart told me about: you couldn't stack books or plates, and it was considered inauspicious to write your name in red.

The bartender dropped off a bowl of colorful puffed cornballs in the center of the table that looked like mutated Fruit Loops. The four of us were taking sips from our sturdy glass tumblers and grabbing at the cornballs with our fingers. Bart was right that I didn't see any hookers there. The bar was pretty empty, and we had a whole extra table to put our coats and scarves down on. There were two mixed couples out on what appeared to be a double date—old Australian businessmen with young Korean girls hanging on their every word. There were a handful of American GIs two tables down from us, but they mostly kept to themselves, making chitchat and glowering at the thick steins of beer on their table.

"If you want to get into a fight in Korea," Paul whispered to me across the table, "just call the American GIs 'Guile.' They can't stand that." The image of Guile, the old Street Fighter character, dressed head-to-toe in camo and sporting a crew cut and a torn tank top sprung to mind, and I couldn't help making the connection to the appropriately dressed men two tables away.

"One day I'd like to see you go up and actually tell them that, Paul," Bart quipped, having heard the joke too many times already.

"Whatever," Paul said, scooting in closer to Sari. "If they were messing with her I'd do something, but I'm not about to get my ass beat for no reason."

"That's sweet, honey," Sari said sarcastically. She fluttered her long eyelids at Paul, and he swatted at them playfully like a cat at a ball of yarn.

I took a long sip from my drink and pounded the empty glass back on the table. It was my fourth drink of the night, and I was definitely feeling it. Koreans compared the chronology of a night out to a train—where each new bar or restaurant in the circuit was like adding another car. Friends competed for the longest train like they were sizing up their manhood. Paul claimed to have had a sixteen-car night once; Bart's all-time high was twenty. We were collectively on four that night with no signs of slowing down. As I put my drink down I suddenly remembered Bart's past history with Rachel and felt like finding out more. I have always had a miserably low tolerance.

"I don't suppose you're dating anyone," I asked, without any context whatsoever, my eyes gazing innocuously up at the ceiling.

Without a second thought, Bart replied coolly: "No, I've been too busy with work to date." I stared down low enough for his eyes to meet mine. "How about you?"

Paul called the waiter back over and ordered another round of whiskey.

"I'm sort of dating Tyra, my co-Fellow in Taigu," I told him, obscuring my face with my hands. "You know, sort of how you were with Rachel."

I peeked out quickly, trying to catch his immediate response. Bart paused for a moment and his face scrunched down hard like he was swallowing a rock.

"Oh," he said, before trailing off into silence. Paul and Sari were having their own conversation for the time being so I thought I would press the issue.

"It was hard, you know, living in such close quarters." The drinks arrived and Bart wordlessly positioned his lips close to the glass. "Like I never *really* knew if it was Rachel herself or the situation," I tried again. "You know what I mean? Like what would it have been like if we were together in the states?" Again, I waited for a response, but Bart was staring off at the two mixed couples gathering their things and getting ready to pay their tab. I thought for a moment about how my mom and dad got together—her Chinese, and he American—and hoped desperately that it didn't look like that.

Bart was looking pointedly at Paul and Sari, trying to segue into their conversation, but they were talking at length about Korean soap operas and how there was always a subplot about someone dying of leukemia. It was obvious that he wanted to drop the subject but I wanted badly to hear his side of things and tried to level with him.

"No, come on, it's okay. Me and Rachel were together last year and she told me—"

"That's not me," Bart blurted out, wiping his mouth with his hand. He bit his lip by accident and let his hand linger there for a moment longer.

Then, very calmly: "I mean, that wasn't me." He looked me dead in the face. "She must have confused me with someone else."

Paul and Sari had finished their conversation and turned to look at us. I was stunned. There was no way that Bart couldn't have known that I knew about the two of them. Early on when we were still getting to know each other, Rachel and I talked in depth about her first year, and I remember how much it surprised me when she told me about Bart—of his crude jokes and boyish antics, and how he never liked to show weakness. I didn't know him very well, but I felt like I learned more about him through her characterization. After a few months, even the loneliness of Taigu wasn't enough to keep them together. Bart started hooking up with one of his students and that was the end of it.

The stigma of a foreign teacher dating a student in a small town like Taigu was immense, and one that Bart went to considerable lengths to downplay. Outside of class, the two of them almost never saw each other in public. When they did, it was late at his house with the tiny incandescent bulb flickering, the blinds drawn, the nightstand shivering. Still, like anything else, it was impossible to keep the relationship from the other foreigners. He had given the girl her English name, and it soon became all she was known by; everyone called her Cherish.

Bart's reputation was damaged irreparably by the whole episode—no one quite looked at him in the same way. They all felt that he had taken advantage of the girl; being found out would have resulted in her expulsion and almost no consequence for Bart.

My situation with Rachel shared some parallels with Bart's, and that's what made me anxious. He and Rachel were never as close as the two of us were, but it hardly mattered. We shared a certain experience in common and neither of us were the kinds of people to talk very openly about it. If we were ranking our experiences, he didn't want competition, and certainly didn't want more people than necessary to find out. It was easy enough, then, to deny it; he knew that as the quintessential host, I was in no position to call him on the truth.

Not long afterward, Bart and Paul ponied up the money for drinks, and we all left the bar. I still felt bad that they were treating me, but in a place like Seoul, their salaries were far more expendable than mine, and I could only really repay them if they came to stay with me in Taigu. As we were walking back down the hill, discomfort grew inside me. Foreigners speaking in accented English came stumbling out of the thinly veiled brothels. There were old mattresses pitched in the narrow alleyways, and piles of steaming trash lay in large, unkempt heaps. The city's homeless were settling in for the night. For some reason, I hadn't noticed any of it when we were walking up.

It was, what Paul later told me, the closest thing Seoul had to a ghetto. All the more shocking was that it was an entirely foreign construction; even poor neighborhoods of Korean locals didn't look half as sleazy. I now understood why the area was so notorious that most locals didn't even go near it. Five drinks in, I again saw the red-outlined doors and crimson curtains and yearned for a flash of skin. Up above them were the stately cathedrals and churches in the overwhelmingly Christian country—another foreign intervention. After dark, the cityscape echoed the scene on the ground—a sea of neon—glowing crosses, burning red into the night.

Back on the street, street vendors were peddling food in small stands covered in plastic to keep in the heat. One of the small vacuum-sealed booths had *tteokbokki,* sticks of rounded rice flour doused in spicy tomato paste, and a generous selection of *sundae*—boiled pig intestines stuffed with cellophane noodles—on a greasy plate. An adjacent booth was selling "hamburgers"—a combination of ground beef and rice formed into thick patties and grilled. It was an interesting concept. Two of the same GIs from the bar—Guile and Guile—were standing by the booth and talking loudly.

"I can't stand this shit," one of them said to the other.

"Get used to it," the other shot back, "we still got four months before we can leave this fucking country."

The burger was probably one of the most normal dishes I'd seen in Korea.

I had only arrived in Seoul three days prior, but Paul insisted on showing me the full spectrum of traditional Korean fare. The four of us tried *ggeopdaegi,* chewy fried pork skin, *beondaegi,* boiled silk worm pupae in a sickening broth, and even *sannakji,* live octopus whose tentacles were still wriggling and squirming as they passed down our throats. There was talk of trying to find *boshintang,* the infamous dog stew served with capsicum and soybean paste, said to improve male virility. Each time, we tried to outdo the other, one-upping our tolerance for the bizarre and, in most cases, vile. I ate it just the same, not wanting to back down, all the while wondering if and when I would get a chance to eat the food I remembered from Korean restaurants in the states.

By the time we made it to Eden, I had all but forgotten about the club. In front of me stood a towering glass pavilion, with swirling multicolored spotlights encircling the sidewalk. The club was on the 34th floor and we needed to be ushered into an elevator to get there. There was a bouncer by the door collecting the entrance fee and a revolving door of entrants dressed in everything from suit jackets to t-shirts. It felt like this weird mix of New York and Beijing—where the former had dress codes and long waits, and the latter didn't care if you were a drunk, sweaty foreigner who barely knew how to dance.

I was wearing something in-between—a button-down shirt and a pair of loose-fitting jeans. Once inside, Paul and I spent the first few minutes surveying the women, trying to guess whose eyelids were real and whose were fake. Paul estimated that half of the girls in Korea had surgery done on their eyes to give them the folded over "double-lid" that Westerners took for granted. Men had their own kind of vanity: they inserted metal rods into their calves to make them taller. There was no stigma around plastic surgery. It was simply something that people did to better themselves, and no one took any issue with that. In China, my students idolized everything Korean—whether it was their music, their beauty, or their fashion. Now that I was there, I was amazed by something different—a society of people obsessed with being something they weren't.

The music was blaring from the twin speakers and I could scarcely hear anything that was going on. Bart ushered both of us over to the bar, and along with Sari, we each did two shots of tequila in quick succession.

"I just want you to have a good time," Bart shouted over the Black Eyed Peas.

He threw the spent lime rind on the floor by the bar, and just as quickly walked off.

I was already woozy and staggering a little when I came in, but by now I had ventured into the large crowd that had gathered at the center of the dance floor. I started practicing the few phrases in Korean that I knew—going up to single-looking female strangers and asking: *Excuse me. Very cute. Sorry. Please. What time is it? Are you happy?*

Imperceptibly, a woman approached me. She was dressed in a black shawl and had a tight wraparound skirt that met a pair of silvery leggings halfway down her thigh. We started dancing close and I wondered if strangers really did things like that on their own accord. She flipped her body in front of me so that her back was pressed up against my chest, and she sunk her hips deep into my thighs, rocking in tune to the beat. I wanted to ask her to leave with me—to go somewhere, anywhere. It didn't sound very much like me, but had I been there long enough, there was no telling what would have happened.

After a couple of minutes, the woman turned around and flashed me a wide grin. With a casualness akin to petting a cat, she reached her hand behind her and slid it slowly and deliberately down my left pant leg. *Strangers didn't just do* that, I reasoned. Then I remembered: *We weren't far from Hooker Hill.*

"I—" I waved my hands in front of my face. "I can't," I said in English before extricating myself and disappearing back into the crowd. As I turned to leave, I saw Bart's face linger for a moment like a buoy above the seething mass. I looked at him just long enough to see him give me this big wink, showing his approval, his own hands pressed close to a stranger whom I couldn't make out. That whole trip he put on his best face for me—gracious, non-judging—hoping that I would do the same for him.

I lost Bart again in the crowd for a while after that. Paul and Sari were dancing on their own and it was late by the time we all came together again. When we were finally ready to go home, Bart and I didn't talk about anything from that evening. For the rest of my time in Seoul, I didn't mention Rachel again or the club or his student from Taigu either. If I were him, I would have probably denied it all too.

REJECTION

Perhaps three or four months into your new life, you may begin to notice yourself showing signs of cynicism and depression. You may begin to build your own set of stories about such things as how inefficient the natives are, how offensively status-conscious they are, or how, as a foreigner, you are always treated as different. You will probably begin to fume over the fact that you are over-charged because you are a Westerner. You may also be getting tired of talking like a three-year-old. You may feel that your scintillating wit has given way to feeling stupid all the time. These feelings may be compounded by the fact that the petty annoyances of the first months don't get better.

From this point you may find your cynicism and depression deepening. You begin to wonder why on earth we ever sent you there and will probably write to us to tell us that you think we need to define what we are doing more succinctly. You will probably find you are nostalgic for the holiday season back home. A big vacation trip will probably come about this time. It will be a terrific trip. Once again every move will be an adventure. It will be a chance to catch your breath and revivify your spirits.

COMPRESSION

It was most certainly a bad day for running. There was something lingering in the air, dark clusters of particulate matter obscuring the bright and sunny view. The mountains had disappeared again, and smoke was billowing out from one of the smokestacks on campus reserved for trash burning. On previous occasions, I fell victim to the ruse—starting out on a slow jog and wondering after a paltry few minutes why I felt winded and found it hard to breathe. We were standing at the edge of the track—Leslie and I—and Leslie was holding a pad and paper in his hands, furiously scribbling new words on it for me to study as he spoke.

There were two tracks at the university. The smaller one was located equidistant between the graduate student dorms and the foreign houses where we lived. In the middle of the track was a makeshift soccer field, fashioned with two sagging goalposts and a broken net. Framed by the track were a number of badminton courts, and when I went running, I often saw my students playing there, always in the individual *danwei* or units that they were grouped into based on major and class year. They smiled at me as I passed, sometimes stopping to ask me if I wanted to play a game with them, or more often, to comment on the clothing I was wearing or how fast they presumed I was running.

The larger 400 meter track was a lot like the small track, except that instead of badminton courts framing it, there were long sets of bleachers stacked lengthwise around its circumference and a hodgepodge of small, one-room offices nestled underneath. The track was much newer, and along with the Olympic-sized swimming pool, was built primarily as a regulation-sized sports complex to host town and countywide track and field meets. But in spite of its newness, the track was poorly maintained. White paint was peeling from the rafters, and bits of gravel kicked up from the asphalt track were mixing in with the Astroturf from the soccer field. As I walked around with Leslie, I felt the shards of gravel nipping at my feet; they always found a way to burrow into my shoes.

It was on our second lap around the track that Leslie told me the story. He was wearing a button-down shirt with glittery purple and silver stripes that he liked to wear during our weekly lessons. I came to think of him in that shirt, in the same way that he undoubtedly identified me by one or the other of the two sweatshirts I wore almost exclusively around campus. It was just something I got used to, that I never thought I would have to take for granted.

Once a year, Shanxi Agricultural University played host to the annual Northern China Agricultural Universities Athletic Meet—the most important sports meet of the year, which brought together the top athletes from across the province. It was a couple weeks before the competition, and the entire school was gearing up for it. Whole classes of students were being pulled out of lecture to do drills and exercises. In addition to competing against other schools, each individual department competed against all of the others, and the results were tallied and displayed in front of the main teaching building for the entire year. Faculty members, including Leslie, were also expected to participate in their own events. It was a great honor to be the winning department, and nobody liked to lose.

"Legend has it that many years ago, one of the foreign teachers competed in this sports meet," Leslie said. He wrote out the word "legend" on his notepad so that I could read the individual characters. 传说: pass down, speak.

"He wasn't as big as you are, but he was fast," he said, striking his hands together to accentuate the last word. "He used to run track at Oberlin and he practiced all the time here too. His main event was the mile. No one at the university could touch him." Leslie stopped and looked out across the track. The cloud of smoke was turning shades of purple in the late evening sun. The school always got the factories going after classes ended at 4:30. I was thankful they didn't power them up in the mornings, but because the late afternoon was the only time we could exercise, we still ended up feeling the brunt of it. Pollution at the university came to have this distinct smell of sulfur and spoiled broccoli.

"So one year, he decides to talk to the athletics coach at the school, and he asks to compete in the sports meet on the school's track team. The coach has seen him run and knows how fast he is and immediately agrees." We started walking again, and we passed by the tiny weight room on campus where the track team practiced. The Plexiglas door was flung open and someone had brought out the two olive-colored mats from inside. A couple of the sprinters were out doing stretches and talking. I recognized two of them, and they gave me a nod and a wave and continued their conversation.

"So it's the day of the big race, and this foreigner wins handily. I mean, just blows past everyone else. He's so fast that he beats all of the Chinese competitors from the other schools." Leslie spoke quickly and it still took me some time to connect all of the foreign words into meaning.

"*Hao niu*," I said triumphantly. "How cool." I learned from Leslie that if something was cool in Chinese, you said it was *niu* or "cow." If it was really cool, you said it was *niu bi*—the "cow's vagina." In the grand scheme of linguistic differences, it wasn't all that strange, so I didn't really question it. I likened it to a more vulgar way of calling something the "cat's meow" in English.

"Maybe for you," Leslie said, "but the other teams were not so happy." Leslie shook his head and laughed. "The coaches all said, 'there's no way this *laowai* is taking home first place and making a fool of us.'" It was this enormous loss of face—a foreigner beating the Chinese at the most important province-wide sports meet of the year.

"So what happened?" I asked.

"What happened," he said, "is that the next year the other schools were prepared for this guy. They knew all about him and this time they were determined not to let him win." I nodded my head and urged Leslie on. Leslie had come to the university twelve years ago and taught Ecological Design. He had the opportunity to do research for a year in California, which is how his English got to be so good. He had been a tutor for generations of Shansi Fellows, and he said that he enjoyed spending time with us because we were like a breath of fresh air, constantly questioning the things that Chinese society simply accepted as fact.

"The other universities banded together," Leslie said. "On the field of six athletes, four of them were tasked with blocking the American and the last one ran ahead for the win." He pulled out the notebook and wrote down another one of the words. 力阻: force, obstruct.

"The officials looked the other way. No one said anything about the result."

I looked at him astonished. "Unbelievable," I said. "So what happened to the winner?"

"He got first place. Everyone cheered. It was a proud day for Inner Mongolia."

"And what ever happened to the foreign teacher," I asked, shaking my head.

"It was his last year at the school so he couldn't have competed again anyway," Leslie said, slowing down his speech. "But ever since then, no foreigner has ever competed in the sports meet." He paused a moment, and then added: "I guess it just wasn't worth it."

Leslie and I had rounded the track three or four more times by then, and it was starting to get dark.

"Let's stop here for today," he said, ripping out the sheet of new vocabulary words and handing it to me. "We'll pick up with this next lesson."

I smiled and thanked him, and he sauntered off in the direction of the faculty apartments where he lived with his wife and son. I folded the paper in my pocket and also headed home, the purple sky masking the way.

Almost everything I knew about Taigu that wasn't passed down from the other foreigners I learned from Leslie. He was young enough that I felt like I could relate to him, but old enough that I was still nervous about our lessons—anxious about being able to retain the vocabulary that we had gone over the previous lesson. My Mandarin was definitely improving, but it still felt like this dragging, arduous process. My listening, especially, was getting pretty good, but I still couldn't express nearly everything that I wanted to say. I was impatient: I wanted to be fluent and be done with it already.

We started off by doing a lot of walking lessons outside. Leslie took a cue from Grant, who liked to teach some of his classes outdoors when the weather was nice. Trotting down the main road, he would shout out the names of things in English—rock, street light, stop sign, awning—and have his students repeat them. I always found it to be a little too slapdash for my style, but it worked pretty well one-on-one with Leslie. The weather was warm, and Leslie used his knowledge of agriculture to point out various plants and trees that lined the streets. There were probably other things that were more useful to learn, but like all good teachers, Leslie excelled when he taught the things he had a genuine interest in. I tried to steal a page from him for my own classes, telling myself: *If I taught to my passions, the rest would follow suit.*

A lot of lessons ended up being a sweeping tour of the campus. I never understood why, but regardless of which direction we went, we always seemed to end up at the track by the lesson's end. It was like clockwork. More often than not, I wore shorts and a t-shirt underneath my sweatshirt so that when we finished our lesson, I could go right to working out. The gym was nothing to write home about, but it sufficed. Nate stumbled upon it one day a couple months into his second year. From the outside, it looked like any one of the anonymous, uniform offices that lined the track. It was only after a little snooping and some delicate buttering up of the track coach that we were given permission to use it.

In truth, it was probably the sorriest excuse for a weight room I'd ever seen— charcoal-covered benches, dilapidated foam mats, and weight plates that looked as if they'd been deep-fried in rust. If you so much as tugged on the locking bolt at either end of the barbell, you could actually separate it from the bar. Past sundown, there was only the faint beam from a single, dangling bulb that illuminated about a quarter of the floor. But bare bones or not, it was a weight room. Grant and I used to go four days a week for two hours at a time to fill that awkward post-class, pre-dinner space.

Occasionally when we went, there were a couple members from the track team practicing inside. It took a while before they got used to our presence there, and even then, there seemed to be an intense fascination with us dressed in tank-tops and shorts in 40 degree weather. Though I was thankful that we could use their room, I was still wary of what they might want of me, and it took me a while to open up to them. Back when we didn't know their names, Grant and I gave monikers to them based on their physical appearance. Two ripped guys—one tall and one short—we decided to brand as Big and Little Rippy. Probably the strongest guy in there we called Tron, who famously quipped in English that, "I don't have a Chinese body; I'm stronger than all of them!"

And then there were lesser known bit players—"ugly shorts guy," "poser strength," and shot put ringer "Andre the Giant," well over six feet tall and at least 250 pounds—the most enormous Chinese man I'd ever seen. A couple of girls on the team were spared the demeaning name treatment—one, a shy tomboy who excelled in the high jump, and another half my size, whom I once saw—much to my simultaneous shock and arousal—squat with 135 pounds draped over her back. They all reminded me a little bit of The Mighty Ducks: a little scrappy, a tad eccentric, but when it came down to it, pretty capable. The same could be said of the weight room itself.

On colder days, Leslie and I had lessons in my living room, or, if Grant was entertaining students there, we moved into my bedroom—me on my bed, and he sitting opposite me on my desk chair. By then my room had already started breathing. Each morning, the wind blew through the wide slits in my windowpanes, slowly inflating and deflating the giant sheet of plastic that I taped over the window to trap the heat.

Without that plastic, it was hard to do much of anything in my room without being wrapped up in blankets. Though it wasn't that cold in the daytime, it got chilly at night, and the school had not yet turned on the university's heat supply. When I first moved to the school, I wasn't thinking about drafty windows or the way the roof curled in on rainy days, or buying metered squares of plastic in bulk. There were too many other unknowns—how I would communicate with people, how I would make friends, how I would learn to teach English. But suddenly there I was— my room, which with its two sets of windows felt like this giant iron lung, alternately compressing and filling the space inside with recycled air.

Leslie described my room differently. We were talking about Liu Xiaobo, the jailed Chinese dissident who had recently won the Nobel Peace Prize. Liu had spent the better part of two decades advocating peaceful political change in the face of relentless hostility on the part of the ruling Chinese Communist Party (CCP), beginning with a hunger strike during the Tiananmen Square protests in 1989. His most recent arrest came after he helped pen a manifesto called Charter '08, which demanded democratic reform that would end the CCP's monopoly on power. I listened as Leslie catapulted into a rant on Chinese censorship. "Any headlines mentioning his name can't be found in state media. It's an atrocity." He wrote the word down in his notepad. 暴行: brutal conduct.

But I understood, too, how people came to accept the censorship. If you only ever heard one news source, you wouldn't know any better not to accept it as the truth. It was as if a padded cell had been built around you, full of all the information you needed to feel sated, and nothing more. Leslie likened that feeling to my room— swathed in plastic, it was like a bubble that the government built around its citizens in order to control their thoughts. There was no movement of ideas—no new air ever made it inside or out.

It was then that it dawned on me—perhaps Leslie could be my project; the conversations I had with him, all the things I learned: I could use that information for good, to transmit to people back home how real, live Chinese citizens lived and thought and engaged with the world. I could be an anthropologist, and Leslie, my subject. He made it a point of making our lessons an open space for dialogue. It seemed, though, that it was only one-way—he sensed how nervous I felt about telling him what I thought about his country and his people. Whenever he asked me a provocative question, he leaned back, put his hand on his chest, and said: "There are no cameras watching us here; you can tell me anything. Trust me."

In the week leading up to the annual Northern China Agricultural Universities Athletic Meet, custodial and maintenance teams were hired to do a cosmetic makeover of the big track. Elderly migrants dressed in fading jeans and wearing dirty bandanas brandished white rollers and repainted the peeling, rust-colored façade. Others were painstakingly removing the tiny bits of gravel from the Astroturf by hand and depositing them into a large pail. A set of younger hired labor was perched on either side of a ladder, replacing Plexiglas windowpanes and hanging up large red banners adorned with inspirational sayings. It didn't matter that in a few weeks' time, the track would return more or less to the way it was. The school was very keen on its image. Everything had to be perfect.

During that time, Leslie got a promotion. He had previously been an adjunct professor at the university, a low-level cadre, but he got promoted to class dean, a top-tier *ganbu* position that had him working closely with school administrators. With the new job came a number of perks, and Leslie was initially very excited about the change. He moved from a shared cubicle into his own office, complete with black leather couch, desk, monitor, and bookcase. His salary increased too—now his wife was able to stay home and raise their son without taking on a night job. Not only that, the new position firmly established him as a card-carrying member of the Communist Party—a marked increase in status and influence.

Pretty soon, I noticed little things begin to change. Leslie's schedule got busy with all sorts of social engagements: banquets over lunch with other Party members, overnight visits to nearby cities—like some kind of indoctrination. They came gradually at first. We started having classes in his office instead of my house. People visited with all sorts of questions in the middle of our lessons; he was taking five or six calls every hour. Then they became too obvious to ignore—a late class here, a rescheduling there. Sometimes he showed up drunk, fresh from a lunchtime banquet—the penetrating scent of *baijiu* still hot on his lips.

The truth was that I didn't know exactly what his new responsibilities were outside of carousing with the other school bigwigs. All I could see was that Leslie looked exhausted—like his defenses were being whittled down. His disposition became more rigid. He stopped wearing the purple and silver striped shirt in favor of collared Oxfords and slacks. He changed the wallpaper on his desktop. Whereas before there was a smiling photo of his wife and son, there was now a single image of the Chinese color guard holding up a flag with three messages in Chinese: "Don't take the initiative!" "Be a good helper!" "Stop thinking for yourself!" Everyone in the Party was supposed to be this single, united voice—this paragon of constancy. The way to the top was paved with vigorous nods of the head and an attitude wholly free of dissent. To join the Party meant giving up a part of oneself. It was one thing to read about it, but another thing to see it unfold.

When I asked Leslie about it, he told me very simply that, "I always want to do things on my own or have my own ideas. But that will get me in trouble. I have to keep reminding myself not to do that." It was the exact opposite of everything I'd ever learned growing up in the states. In my head, the quotes across Leslie's computer were so self-consciously irreverent that I thought it was a joke. But I could tell that Leslie was only half-laughing. He warned me at one of our lessons: "Don't try to be individual." Again, he wrote down the characters for me to see. 个性: one character, one quality.

We were talking in one class about the Cultural Revolution and Leslie stopped me in the middle of a thought.

"You don't understand," he told me. "Mao was not a dictator like Stalin."

"A what," I asked.

"A dictator." Leslie wrote down the characters on his notepad. 独裁者: sole judicator. "Mao was an honest man who believed he could help the people. Stalin was a killer." He made his hands in the shape of a gun, reeling back as he pulled on the trigger.

I furrowed my brow. "But Mao, he also killed people," I said, surprising myself with my own candor.

"Those people died of starvation," Leslie said. "At that time, there was no food, no resources." He paused, seeing a wave of grief pass across my face. It was like his body was screaming: *I know there's something more here, but I can't say it just now.* "China was different then," he managed, still a bit unconvincingly. "Things have improved a lot." He let his head slump down from his shoulders, and breathed out deeply through his mouth. "Let's stop here, alright," he said quietly, ripping out the loose-leaf sheet. It was like there was so much I wanted to tell him, and yet I didn't quite remember how.

On the morning of the annual Northern China Agricultural Universities Athletic Meet, the entire school was in a frenzy. The bleachers surrounding the big track were packed, and students had woken up early to get a glimpse of the once-yearly event that was probably the most exciting thing they would experience all semester. It kicked off with a series of performances by a group of current students: fan dances, *tai qi* exercises. After remarks by the headmaster and the party secretary of the college, it was on to the races.

The student athletes were up first. As an agricultural school, Shanxi Agricultural University had not historically been a contender for any of the big races. Its only hope was with the Exercise Science students, who were corralled almost exclusively from members of the track and field team. In the heat of the midmorning sun, The Mighty Ducks were up to play. Classmates in the crowd applauded and culled in a chorus of *JIA YOU!* Andre the Giant took home first in the shot-put. Little Rippy won second in the 400 meter. Their teammates cheered and exchanged high-fives when the races were finished. None of the others placed.

Legend had it that the sports meet had changed dramatically over the past several years. Nowhere was this truer than when it came to events specifically for the faculty. Originally conceived as a measure of physical ability and toughness, the meet had devolved over time, with some of the original events being phased out on account of being too strenuous. The school realized that many of its staff and professors were no longer fit enough to run a five-mile race, so the longer runs were scrapped in favor of shorter ones. Hurdles were done away with altogether on account of being too dangerous. And field events like the pole vault and the javelin throw were replaced with the "Frisbee toss," even though most Chinese had no conception of how to even throw a Frisbee.

Leslie lamented the change, noting that the whole thing felt more like a carnival with streamers and games than an actual athletic competition. But he said it was ultimately for the best. Though he was an avid badminton player, he cited that most faculty didn't engage in physical activity of any kind, so when you took someone who was used to sitting down at a desk for eight hours a day and suddenly made him run long distances, there were bound to be accidents. Still, the school kept up the bastardized tradition of the sports meet for no ostensible reason other than because it was what administrators had done in the past, and no one wanted to be the first to petition for its repeal.

In spite of all the scaling back, the changes appeared to have little impact on the competitive spirit of the meet. If anything, they seemed to make the participants even more cutthroat. With the distances shrunk to a fraction of the length, everyone believed they were capable of coming in first. Distinguished and upright faculty were not exempt from the overwhelming lawless attitude of Chinese citizens: in order to win, they were willing to do everything in their power—scrape, push, and jostle—for the medal. Leslie told me about one teacher a few years ago who, on the last leg of a relay race, lunged and fell. The whole of his weight came crashing down on his left knee, shattering his fibula. The school responded by stationing an ambulance on the near side of the field every year after that.

The Ecological Design faculty went head-to-head with Botany, Animal Husbandry, and Water Resource Management in a 100 meter dash that ended in participants sweeping up a baton sticking straight out of the ground to claim victory. From the bleachers, I watched Leslie line up at the blocks and heard the shot from the starting gun. He had a good jump on the competition, but the other teachers came down hard. In the final seconds, Leslie lunged for the baton and grabbed a hold of it, but in the process, he was knocked down and trampled by one of the other runners. A wide gash cut along his upper forearm, and he lay on the ground bleeding for a time before medical personnel came to investigate.

A hush came over the crowd as they waited to hear the extent of the injury. The other participants—his colleagues—shifted their weight awkwardly on the field, unsure of what to do. But after a few seconds, Leslie got to his feet and the bleachers erupted in more cheers, this time even from the opposing team. The medical personnel carried him carefully to the other side of the field where they applied bandages to his arm and wrist. Leslie waved to the crowd with his uninjured hand, holding his bloodied arm crookedly behind his back, careful not to let anyone see.

When it was time to pose for photos on the winner's stand that the school had set up to imitate the Olympics, Leslie stood valiantly at the center spot, looking out at his colleagues and the rest of the crowd. But before the photographer could snap off the photo, one of the school administrators pointed to Leslie's shirt, noting a small clump of blood that had stained his white shirt red from the injury. Almost instinctively, he reached into the crowd, and asked to borrow a jacket from one of the students looking on. He handed it to Leslie, and Leslie slipped his bandaged arm carefully inside of it, zipping it up over his white shirt. Years later, no one would recall the outfit change. It was only the photo they would remember, and nothing else.

(INDIA)

INSOMNIA

"I'm sorry to tell you this, but Insomnia is closed for the evening." The concierge was dressed in a fitted jacket and wore a matching set of tassels on his shoulder pads that I thought native only to London bellhops. The man had a demure, bashful look about him, and it took considerable effort for him to meet my eyes.

The three of us were stationed in the front lobby of the Taj Mahal Palace Hotel, probably the most opulent and iconic hotel in all of Mumbai. Two years prior, it had been the site of a series of terrorist attacks that left over 150 people dead and millions of dollars in repairs. The front of the building was still draped in mesh construction material and there was only a single barricaded entrance, guarded by a bevy of armed guards. In order to get in, we had to put our things on a conveyor belt metal detector, and the bearded guards patted us down like we were going through airport security. Everything about it felt like a stark contrast to the indomitable disorder of the rest of India.

It was probably the last place in the city we expected to find ourselves, considering we were operating on a strict budget and had only been sleeping in proper beds for half of the journey. In our over-ambitiousness, we were pushing to a new town or city every two days, which meant one day was spent at a hostel and the second was encamped on an overnight train on our way to the next destination. It felt like this perpetual sleep debt, without enough time to ever catch up. Despite coming from China, I couldn't believe how unfathomably large India seemed—the entire country shaped like this bloated kidney, with trains like arteries that pumped blood cells from end to end.

"There must be some mistake," Kyla started in, holding the *Lonely Planet: India* firmly in her hands. She had the look of someone who had come too far just to fail now.

"Is it because this is a weekday?" she asked, tightening the forest green scarf around her hair and rounding her shoulders. She paged through the guidebook and landed on the "Entertainment" section for Mumbai. Sure enough, Insomnia was front and center on the page—*For Bollywood star-spotting, ultrachic Insomnia remains the place to be seen dropping some serious dough.* In a city renowned for its nightlife, it was the only club listed in the book that was open past midnight.

"No, Insomnia is closed every evening," the concierge replied in a low, even-keeled voice. "It's been permanently shut down." The lobby of the Taj Mahal was considerably quieter than we had seen it earlier that day. Rachel and I, each desperately seeking a decent toilet, had come in to escape the crowds outside. The Taj Mahal was located right by a port overlooking the Arabian Sea and locals were peddling photos by the bay and boat tours to see some of the surrounding sights. It didn't matter that it was a Monday and nearly all of the advertised attractions were closed. People seemed so desperate to get us into a boat and paddle us out to the ocean that it only came as an afterthought that there would ostensibly be nothing there to see.

Kyla turned back to Rachel and me with a look of equal parts disbelief and fury.

"What do you mean it's 'permanently shut down,'" she asked with a sneer. She cocked her head back and tersely set her hands akimbo. She ripped the "Entertainment" page out of the *Lonely Planet* and dangled it in front of his face.

"See here," she said, pointing at the hours. "Monday through Saturday 8 PM - 3 AM." Rachel and I looked at each other and then over at Kyla and the concierge. She flashed me a tight smile and held out her hand, trying to diffuse the tension. I could tell that she was worried about me—knowing how I generally reacted to lapses in planning—and that I could lose my cool at any moment.

But it wasn't just everyday failures that bothered me. India was a special case—with one spectacular failure after another that never seemed to stop. The simple fact that we had made it that far felt like victory enough. Ironically, being at the Taj Mahal Palace Hotel was perhaps the only time that I hadn't felt the crushing sense of defeat. At the very least, there was a dedicated newspaper stand stocked with shelves of foreign magazines and plenty of boutique clothing stores for quiet window-shopping. Better still, there was the bathroom I remembered from that morning—with real marble sinks, sprigs of potpourri and a bathroom attendant who dispensed tough, woven towels as liberally as if they were paper.

"Your book is mistaken," the concierge piped up, finally starting to show some color. "Insomnia has been closed for seven years." A gust of salty warm air came wafting through the front door, and by now everyone who was in the lobby—businessmen still suffering from jetlag, young couples dressed in black—had turned to watch the commotion.

Kyla burst out laughing. "Seven years," she exclaimed, holding back the anger in her voice. "Seven years, really." She turned and backed away from the concierge desk. "Well, looks like *Lonely Planet* was wrong," Kyla said, throwing her hands in the air. And then, just for good measure: "What else is fucking new?"

All day, the three of us had been wearing the nicest clothes we brought on the trip. Insomnia, home to Bollywood elite, would be expecting us in only our finest backpacker duds, we reasoned. I had on a white collared shirt with French sleeves that I had folded up the length of my forearm. Kyla was wearing a wrap-around *sarong* dress that may have been native to India. Rachel had on a pair on dangly earrings and white pants. We each still had a pair of dark Aviator sunglasses looped around our shirt collars even though it was well past sundown.

Early the next morning we would be parting ways—Kyla back to Madurai, a middle-sized city in southern India where she had been living for the past four months, and Rachel and I to the north to Delhi for a day before a connecting bus to Dharamsala. It was the same cyclical pattern—one day in, next day out. I had heard incredible things about the north—about the mountain ranges that seemed to sprout up from the sea, the quaint isolation of the rural countryside. It would be much cooler up there—long jacket weather. Meanwhile, both of my arms were maculated in mosquito welts. *Surely anywhere else was better than this*, I reasoned. Our train ride was 28 hours long; Kyla's was 35.

Our plan had been to save money and skip the cost of a hotel room. Considering that we wouldn't have had much time to sleep anyway, we figured it made sense to forego the cost of one night's hotel stay and instead go out on the town, using the money we would have otherwise spent on club fees and fancy drinks. Under most circumstances, in India, drinking for women was considered social suicide, and this was one of the few venues to do it. Though Rachel was just visiting, Kyla would be living in India for the next two years—long enough not to want to ruin her reputation. Neither Rachel nor I had had a drink since we left China nearly ten days ago. By the time we got to Mumbai, it was all I could think about.

With no hotel to go back to after we checked out that morning, we spent the rest of the day sightseeing. On the street, noisy hawkers shouted out prices for sandals, batteries, tailor-made suits. Mumbai boasted slick Western hotels and restaurants right alongside crumbling, disintegrating shantytowns. Streets were flooded with people, carts, and cows. Everywhere we went, kids had their hands cupped in front of their chests, pointing despairingly at their mouths. I saw a man selling *lassis* out of the dilapidated shell of a storefront. I plopped a five-rupee coin down on the table. He blended the yogurt concoction and poured it into a tall tin cup that rested mouth-down on the counter. I lapped up the milky fruit mixture, glistening and translucent in the afternoon sun.

With the only place presumed opened past midnight now conveniently closed, we scrambled to think of a plan B.

"So, what now?" Rachel asked, deferring to Kyla, our resident expert on India. She was on a Shansi Fellowship doing what we all did in Taigu, but in Madurai. We'd met during training the previous winter and like all of the other Fellows, developed the kind of rapport where we wanted to go out of our way to see each other in our respective countries. We were her first visitors to India, and, since she was also on winter break, we decided to travel together around the country, starting from the north and making a wide arc to the west. Classes for her started earlier than we had to leave, so Rachel and I were going to travel solo for the last bit of time before returning to China. Despite having never met before, the two of them hit it off surprisingly, almost unbelievably well.

Kyla checked her watch—it was a little after 1 AM.

"I've never had to do this before," Kyla said plaintively. "Maybe there's somewhere here we could stay for a few hours."

She drifted back towards the concierge, smoothing out the decorative pattern of her dress.

"Excuse me, sir, but do you know any place that's open right now we could go to?" she asked entreatingly, as if it were the first time approaching him. She had an attitude that seemed to suggest, *Sorry I lost my cool back there. What's say we put our differences behind us and start fresh?*

The concierge stared back at her and shook his head from side to side in the very Indian way that I came to despise. It suggested neither deference nor admonishment.

"We have a restaurant upstairs on the second floor," he said. "It's open all night."

"Thank you," Kyla mustered and turned to walk back towards Rachel and me, who had migrated to the couches in the front lobby. Already we could tell that the staff was getting suspicious that we might set up shop right there for the evening. "I must warn you though," the concierge called back. "The menu, it is quite expensive."

Kyla offered an Indian head bobble of her own. There were dark circles under her eyes and beads of sweat clung to her forehead.

"It's worth a shot," she said, and the three of us made our way upstairs.

The hotel restaurant was large and well lit, with tapestries adorning each wall and decorative silk cloths spread over the furniture. We chose a table by the far side of the room, and, at our insistence, the waiter brought over a bottle of 400 rupee water—their absolute cheapest, which was roughly 40 times the street price. We each had our luggage stacked in a pile between the table and the wall. At the time, I still had no idea how to travel and was dragging around the big rolling black suitcase that was utterly futile to use on India's uneven, crowded sidewalks. Besides, the mechanism that lifted the handle had broken, so in a pinch I carried the 50-pound behemoth as I saw others do—placed squarely on top of my head, my arms stabilizing it from either side.

"So, what did you think about Mumbai," Kyla asked, managing a smile that was almost apologetic.

"It was my idea to go to Mumbai," I proffered. "I can take the heat for it."

"It wasn't so bad," Rachel jumped in. "We had those great pastries this morning."

"They *were* great," Kyla shot back. "God, I would kill for a Western bakery in Madurai," she said. "There's only one café near my apartment and the coffee's not even good."

"Well we don't even *have* coffee in Taigu," Rachel said, quick to respond. "Apparently China doesn't believe in coffee."

"I think that's because people believe it gives them diarrhea," I said.

"Are you sure they said *diarrhea?*"

"Yes," I said, "I'm fairly certain."

"I feel like it was something else," Rachel said, fumbling for the words. "Headache, maybe? Or nausea? Yes, definitely nausea."

She nodded her head at Kyla. I was too tired to argue about it. Sometimes I just wished Rachel would agree with what I said so we could both move on.

Rachel and I were dating then, and we had decided it would be nice to take a trip together away from Taigu and away from China. What we should have probably been choosier about, though, was where exactly we would go. Traveling as a couple within a group of three was hard enough when the other two people already knew each other, and you weren't in a place that, against all expectations, was even more defiantly chaotic than where you'd started. Rachel and I were fighting a lot— more than we ever did in Taigu.

The waiter came back to check on us, and, feeling guilty that we had just bought a bottle of water to split between three people, Kyla ordered a bowl of onion and cheddar soup that came with bottomless servings of Italian bread. Considering that we still had four hours left until our train, it was a prescient move. Our train was leaving first but Kyla was adamant about seeing us off, making sure that we made it safely aboard before heading back home to Madurai. She did an extraordinary job of taking care of us on the trip, trying to make everything as painless as possible. Admittedly though, there was a lot that was outside of her control.

"I'm sorry we never got to see you in Madurai, Kyla," I said, in between bites of bread. Kyla offered her soup up to Rachel and me, and I was dipping the bread gingerly in the creamy orange of the bowl.

"It's fine," she said. "You guys would have probably hated it anyway."

"Why's that?" Rachel asked.

"It's just a shitty place to live," Kyla said. "It's hot all the time, there are mosquitoes everywhere. I don't know, every day just feels like this enormous struggle." She took a deep breath and set the spoon down next to her soup bowl.

"But the worst thing is that it's just really isolating." She tore at a piece of bread with both hands. "I'm lonely all the fucking time."

Kyla's was the only Shansi site without co-Fellows. She lived in an apartment on campus of the women's university where she taught, and men weren't even allowed to stay on the premises past sundown. I wasn't sure how many other foreigners lived in the city, but she mentioned only that she had one friend. He was an American named Garb who was on a research Fulbright and lived ten minutes away by motorized scooter. She told us that he was a serious man, about ten years her senior, who was meticulously neat and rarely left his apartment. They usually ended up seeing each other about once a week—always at her request. As a man, he was the only one she could ask to buy her alcohol.

"That's really tough," Rachel said. "I can't imagine being out here all alone."

"And it's not like I'm not trying," Kyla said. "All my students are in high school and it's weird whenever I try to see them outside of school. Half the time my kids don't even show up for class and I just end up watching *Speed Racer* on the AV room projector by myself and crying."

Kyla unwrapped and redid the scarf around her hair. She kept her long hair wrapped and knotted at the top of her head, and covered in a tight coif so as not to draw any further attention to herself.

I thought about what it might have been like to live in Madurai alone—to not have any friends for miles, to not spend time with my students outside of class. I considered having to be so dependent on the shaky internet to carry correspondences across an ocean back home. It all seemed unthinkable. It was true that there were also few foreigners in Taigu—arguably many fewer than in Madurai because at least tourists came there to see the Meenakshi temple, which attracted 15,000 visitors a day. But the foreigners that were in Taigu I was very lucky to have. We were all lucky to have each other.

Hours passed sluggishly in the large, bright room. We ordered another bottle of water, and a few other stragglers were seated in the restaurant. A group of rowdy teenagers—presumably the sons and daughters of diplomats staying at the hotel—had congregated over in the far corner. A man dressed in all black sat with a cup of coffee and yesterday's *Times of India*. I had a newspaper propped up in front of me too that I alternated between trying to actually read and using as a cover to nod off before being startled back awake. I had slept exceptionally poorly on the train to Mumbai from Udaipur—an aberration, considering I could normally sleep anywhere—and I couldn't imagine being more tired. The teenagers were talking loudly about what kind of car their chauffeur drove, and I wanted to blame them for keeping me awake. I didn't feel at all like talking.

"I'm so not looking forward to going back to Taigu," Rachel moaned, breaking the momentary lull.

Kyla yawned and stretched, wringing her hands over her head. "Why, what's Taigu like?" she asked, rubbing her eyes and adjusting the pillow behind her.

"Taigu is Taigu," she said. Considering that Kyla had never been, I didn't know what Rachel was getting at.

"Little things," she said. She took a sip of the soup—now considerably cooler—that was still sitting on the table. "We don't have any privacy. Our water shuts off at 10:00 every night. We can lose electricity for days." She looked casually up at the ceiling and then down again at Kyla. "I don't know, at this point it's hard for me to rationalize why I'm still there."

I ate the last piece of bread and called on the waiter to bring another basket. *If only there were also refills on the soup*, I thought, *this would* really *feel like The Olive Garden.*

"I hear that," Kyla said, her voice regaining its earlier composure. "Plus being the only woman—"

"Don't even get me started on that!" Rachel said, placing her hand at the center of the table.

"Being a woman in India is murder," Kyla said. "I have this stalker who follows me around town every time I leave the campus. Half the time, I'm afraid to leave my house."

"That's miserable," Rachel said. "I tell these guys all the time how hard it is to be the only foreign woman in Taigu. The other foreigners, they just feel so insular, you know? I feel like I want to branch out, do my own thing."

Kyla and Rachel went back and forth like that for a while. They were speaking with such quickness that I couldn't even get a word in if I wanted. A lot of the ten days together went like that. Everywhere we went together, the two of them gallivanted ahead and I kept lagging behind. It was almost like I didn't need to be there, that I could have orchestrated this trip and then vanished just as quickly from the picture. I had come to India primarily to see Kyla, but I felt like I hadn't even had a chance to really talk to her. I conceded, in the end, that it was probably a good thing—something like bonding, the two of them trying to outdo the other's misery.

A foreign couple sat down at the other end of the room. They were both about our age, and it looked like they were at the restaurant for the same reason we were. It was like being part of a divided family, its two factions sitting at opposite ends of a long table, not talking to one another at all.

"I don't have many people I can talk to about stuff," Rachel went on. "I tell my friends back home that I've only got him!" she said, pointing her thumb in my direction. She laughed a lilting, high-pitched laugh that quickly morphed into something else.

Just then, my head started to hurt and I felt an eerie pain in my stomach. Kyla was probably right when she warned me about eating raw fruit on the street, or of the yogurt that marinated unrefrigerated for hours before becoming mango *lassi*. A loud gurgling noise erupted from my chest cavity. So much for my iron stomach. I decided to hold off on more bread.

"I've got to pee," Kyla started, getting up from her chair. "I'll be right back." She walked towards the door, gesticulating with the waiter about which direction to turn down the hallway. Rachel sat silently at the table, like she were patiently awaiting her next instructions.

"So, how are you," I asked, as if we had just seen each other for the first time. She looked at me cross-eyed. "Fine," she said. "Why, you?"

"Not great," I replied, not bothering to look up from the table. "This whole place, it's making me crazy."

"What, you mean the restaurant?"

"This conversation, still having to sit here like this." I paused for a minute. Then, somewhat caustically, I added: "Have we even had a real conversation since we've been in this country?"

Rachel mulled the question over in her head. "I don't know. I mean Kyla, she's always... And besides, I don't get that many opportunities like this anyway."

I nodded my head, careful to show empathy.

"I just get sick of talking about the same things," I said. "The way we're just rehashing everything we hate about our lives. It gets tiring after a while. Almost like having to relive it."

I shot her a look that at once suggested entreaty and apology.

"Well, how else will it improve," she asked, catching me off-guard. "I *need* to talk to someone about these things."

"Well, then we might as well be open about everything," I mouthed.

"Okay," Rachel said. "You first."

"I want to get out of this country. I never thought I'd say this, but I want to go back to China."

Rachel glared at me like a teacher who had just caught her student cheating.

"Now come on, you don't really mean that."

"How do you figure?"

"There are so many things to like about India."

"See, this is exactly what I'm talking about," I grumbled noisily.

"What?"

"You know, just once it would be great if you could sympathize with me—to say something like, 'This sucks, but it's okay because we're going to get through it together.'" I looked around the room, making sure that none of the snickering teenagers were watching.

"Really, I don't do that?" she asked inquisitively. "Because I *really* feel like I do."

Kyla came back from the bathroom, and scooted back up in her chair.

"We should probably start heading out," she said, glaring at the clock on the wall. "It's almost 5:00 now."

We graciously paid the tab, gathered up our things, and noiselessly moved to the exits.

Figuring that we had already splurged on the restaurant, we decided that we might as well take a taxi to the train station too. I was thankful to have momentarily postponed the sensation of riding in an Indian train. I readied myself for what the next day would entail—the train station being a disaster, men literally hanging out of windows because of the heat, a grid of rusted metal bars that felt like a prison. Even though it was locked to the sleeper bunk, I always worried that someone would steal my suitcase in the middle of the night. I don't know why—I never thought about it in China. I found myself missing the trains in China, where at least after a ragged night's sleep, someone would wake you up and tell you it was time to get off in the morning.

When our cab arrived, the train station was swarming with people sleeping outside on towels and blankets right on the street. An upshot of Mumbai's heat was that it had ostensibly created a solution for the city's homeless population. Right before we boarded, Rachel and I stocked up on the usual train supplies—two big bottles of water, a bag of "Magic Masala" potato chips, and a packet of digestive biscuits. I threw in a second sleeve of the biscuits just to be sure. As I turned to leave, I gripped Kyla tightly by the side of the train, unsure of the next time I would see her again. I whispered to her softly so that none of the Indians around us could hear.

"India, I mean, this whole country. Is it always like this?"

"Worse," she said, not needing a moment to think. "You two aren't usually here."

The doors closed, and the train pulled slowly out of the station. It was still pitch dark, and only a few lampposts out at street level and the light emanating from within the train lighted the station. Kyla waved at us through the window, watching as we stowed our bags underneath the bunks and sat down on the bottom cot. She started with a slow walk, then moved into a light jog, and finally ran at a full sprint along the side of the train. She was smiling and waving until the bitter end, when finally our faces retreated from view. I saw the tears, slow and heavy, trickling down her face as she watched, unable to turn away. I thought about it—Rachel and I on the train for 28 hours, Kyla going back to Madurai alone. I could tell she felt it too—nothing would ever be that easy after that.

BOMB SCARE

EXT DAY: KMT ARMY BARRACKS (SUMMER 1940)

A HIGH ANGLE of the KMT ARMY BARRACKS in bright daylight. There are at least 50 KMT guards armed with rifles and wearing full gear encircling the compound. CLOSE VIEW of KMT GUARD strapping a bomb to the chest of FOREIGN DIPLOMAT.

> FOREIGN DIPLOMAT
> A real bomb? All of these men and not one of them can disarm it? I don't want to be blown to kingdom come!

KMT GENERAL laughs and shakes his head at FOREIGN DIPLOMAT, revealing a long, crooked smile.

> KMT GENERAL
> Relax, of course it's not real! We just want the CCP to understand that this is a serious threat. We have to give the illusion that it's real.

> FOREIGN DIPLOMAT
> Ah, I see. So then it's just to build the atmospheric tension?

> KMT GENERAL
> Precisely.

FOREIGN DIPLOMAT pauses and looks beseechingly at KMT GENERAL.

> FOREIGN DIPLOMAT
> By the way, after this is all over, how will I get home?

KMT GENERAL
You remember that woman you met?
Medusa? She will make sure you get
home safely.

FOREIGN DIPLOMAT
Medusa… the terrifying woman with
nine snakes in her hair? Got it!

Before we even had to read it, I had a bad feeling about the plot. Grant and I were each sitting on one of the two beds in an upscale, two-star hotel room, scanning over the script. The Chinese Nationalist Party (KMT), under Chiang Kai-shek, was in a last ditch effort to push Mao and the Chinese Communist Party (CCP) from its few remaining strongholds around the country's major urban centers. It was set shortly after the Second Sino-Japanese War, a long and bloody battle that gained infamy following the Japanese capture and subsequent razing of the Chinese capital Nanjing.

Grant finished reading through it first and helped me with spot-translations of some of the more difficult words. I tried to make sense of the meaning.

The casting and assistant directors, dressed in slacks and button-down shirts, carefully slid out of their suit jackets to eat their prepackaged lunches. The mirror directly facing me was blanketed in yellow sticky notes, and there was a big red phone mounted on the wall next to it. It looked like a stage prop from a science fiction movie.

"Now, out loud," the casting director said in between bites of baby bok choy. Grant took a deep breath and looked like he was about to start extemporizing right off the page, but the assistant director cut him off.

"First, memorize it," the assistant director said, covering the phone's mouthpiece momentarily with his hand.

The script that we were reading was for an episode of the Chinese television drama 尖刀队, or Tip of the Dagger, then in its seventh season. Prior to this audition, I had never heard of the show. My students later told me that the drama was a period piece, not dissimilar from the hundreds of other docudramas and biopics that the

Chinese government commissioned. China's wartime history seemed to serve as a conduit for the country's nationalist fervor.

Every fall, students at the university were forced to participate in military training—marching drills, hand-to-hand combat, and simulated battle scenarios. In the evenings, they were seated in the center of the big track to watch propaganda films intended to raise their nationalist ethos. The most important aim of the training was to instill love for one's country and to create a community of young people rallying around a common cause. The students struck me themselves as actors in some kind of overblown production—dough-eyed freshmen donning military fatigues and fake rifles and shouting off memorized slogans well into the night.

Grant and I corroborated our translations with the casting director to make sure we had gotten them right. The script functioned like most of the other serialized programs about the war I had seen in China. In it, the brave and heroic Communists ultimately outdo the avaricious and scheming Nationalists. It made for the classic underdog story: the CCP—only through incredible sacrifice and perseverance— prevailed in the end, and modern-day China was all the stronger and mightier because of it. They always made a point of injecting the Japanese into the story—but only in long, drawn-out sequences where Japanese soldiers were slaughtered by the thousands by brave Communists.

The CCP was portrayed as singlehandedly fighting this two-front war—one against the Nationalists and the other against the Japanese. What all of the biopics failed to mention, though, was the fact that the Communists were losing the war badly, and that it was only with the help of foreign intervention that Japan ultimately surrendered. In the script, the foreign diplomat was depicted as little more than a moronic half-wit. Naïve and corruptible, he gets coerced by the evil Nationalists to work as a spy against the CCP. At the end of the season, the spy realizes that the bomb is in fact real—that the Nationalists had lied to him and were using him as a suicide bomber—and the bomb is detonated. Then there is this massive explosion where the diplomat's body is ravaged in unsympathetic, gruesome detail, and blood is splattered in thick crimson streaks across the set.

It didn't matter that the whole series was historically inaccurate. China writes its own history and millions of young students across the country are subjected to it and accept it as fact. As a teacher, part of me felt guilty—that I had some responsibility to the truth, or at the very least an obligation to portray both sides of the conflict. But at the end of the day, no moralizing could keep me from wanting to do it. I had immense trouble turning down opportunities, and it didn't help, that there was only one foreigner role, and between Grant and I, only one of us would get it.

We practiced the lines out in the hallway in loud, exasperated breaths, trying to nail the drama of the scene. After a few minutes, the casting director called us back in to do a run through with him reading the lines for the KMT official. Grant went first. Since we first arrived in Taigu, Grant had always had a much better grasp of written Mandarin than I. He could read books at a slow but manageable pace while I could scarcely connect the strokes on a series of town and city names. Speaking, though, was definitely his weak point; after just four months, I felt like I had gotten to the point where I spoke nearly as naturally as he did in conversation.

The moment Grant started in with the bomb line, I could tell that he was nervous. He kept repeating parts of it two or three times before getting it all out, and his intonation was all off. "I don't want to be blown to kingdom come," Grant sputtered, sounding more like a comatose patient than an anxious man on the brink of destruction.

Eventually, the casting director let him read the lines from the script; I wasn't sure if Grant was even aware that he had lost face. He finished the dry run feeling confident and satisfied, and I was up next. Maybe it was the extra time I had to prepare or a secret, dormant yearning for the big screen, but my lines came out flawlessly. If it came down to that audition, I thought, there would be no contest. But much to my surprise, the two men conferenced for a time out in the hallway leaving Grant and me to stew nervously in the room, not saying a word. Finally, the casting director returned and said: "I will take you both to meet the director."

Two weeks earlier, two students innocuously dropped by my house and approached me with the possibility of doing acting work for a Chinese film company. The next day, on a walk back from dinner, I got a shadowy call from a woman with instructions to meet her at one of the girl's dormitories on the far side of campus to go over the details.

The woman was in her late 50s with horn-rimmed glasses and wavy salt-and-pepper hair, the kind you'd expect to see in a period piece about 1950s America.

We met in the tiny rectangular cubicle where she worked and also slept at night on a fold-down Murphy bed. On the wall behind the desk was a huge switchboard with little toggles demarcating individual dorm rooms and a giant lever that hung from the side like it were a slot machine. The switchboard controlled electricity to the entire dorm and she told me with an almost malicious satisfaction that it was her job to enforce the curfew and to administer lights-out by pulling down on the lever at 10:30 PM every night.

The way the light switch lady explained it, the TV executives arrived in Taigu and through a distant familial connection first went to her to ask if there were any foreign teachers at the university. Like other side jobs in China, any agreement would be off the books, so no one thought to ask the school's administration for permission. I inferred that she then outsourced that job to some of the girls in the building who knew someone who knew someone who knew someone who was in one of our English classes, which eventually led to me. I imagined that the film company would pay her a commission if she were able to identify the right candidate, and, so, she had a lot riding on our conversation.

The light switch lady offered me a seat by the desk. I told her that none of the foreign teachers at the university had any acting experience but that we were willing to hear out the company's offer. The series was looking for one role—male, foreign, and who needed to be able to understand basic Mandarin. The part called for at least four separate trips to Qixian, a county seat in the neighboring town about twenty minutes from Taigu. Though the parts were relatively small, each shoot could last up to an entire day—eight to twelve hours. She said that the director was willing to pay 600 *yuan* per day—about 90 dollars—including transportation to and from our houses and meals on set. It was about a fourth of our month's salary; with four trips we could nearly double our income.

Besides Rachel, any one of us would have pretty much fit the part. I thought about telling the others and what kind of reaction I would get. Nate didn't do any jobs outside of his teaching duties mostly due to sheer apathy, and Luca didn't know enough Chinese to keep up with the script. Even if there had been a female part available, Rachel was too busy those days tending to Mumu, the demure white cat she had cared for since her first year, who had been having some medical issues of late. I knew that the directors would not have been interested in Jerry, a full Korean, who would more likely have been mistaken for Chinese than American. In the end, I decided not to mention it at all. I told the light switch lady that I would do it, and headed back home, hoping no one would ask where late on a routine Sunday night I could possibly have been.

On the day I left for Qixian, the light switch lady called every half-hour to confirm and reconfirm the audition. Mumu was slated to undergo surgery at the small animal hospital on campus. Complications arose after her first pregnancy when doctors had her tubes tied to prevent further births. However, it soon became clear that against reason she had gotten pregnant again. The doctors had botched the neutering such that the newborn kittens were stillborn, but instead of passing through her, had stayed lodged in her abdomen like a tumor about the size of a child's fist. Doctors worried that without surgery the lump could keep growing until it eventually killed her from the inside. Rachel was concerned that the new set of doctors—Master's students still training to be vets—would be just as ineffective as the last, but she had no other choice.

"I want you to be here," she told me the night before, in bed. "Just in case."

The next morning, when the directors came over, Grant was also at the house. He was as curious about the opportunity as I was and the directors were more than happy to accommodate his request. So he hopped in the van with the light switch lady, the two assistant directors, and me, and we drove the twenty minutes down winding country roads to Qixian. All I could think about was how presumptuous Grant had been to invite himself along and how clueless he was to the fact that this was *my* experience and that I wanted to have it alone.

Four months in, Grant and I were getting along better than we had in the first week, but not by much. My biggest fear when I was going through teacher training in the states was not living in rural China or not being able to speak Mandarin, but of having to live with Grant in the same house for two years. Our personalities clashed on just about every level, and the same issues kept creeping up: how boastful he was, his oblivious lack of tact, how he always needed to be right.

Before we met the director, Grant and I were taken into the dressing and makeup room. There were long racks of shirts, jackets, and slacks, a plethora of other kinds of props—bandoliers, helmets, rifles—and a large pile of pre-bloodied sheets in a sack at the front of the room. The whole place was encased in glass and was staffed by two young, chipper women who started pulling articles off of hangers the minute we walked in.

The two women helped Grant and I change into period. We each wore identical outfits: white collared shirt, black slacks with a belt, black loafers, vest, Western suit jacket, tie. After we changed into our clothes the women quietly applied make-up—mostly just eye shadow and blush—and made a side part in our hair with a wad of gel. I felt already like I had aged by at least a decade. One of the women pulled out a cardboard sheet with a swath of fake mustaches and tried them on me one-by-one. None of them seemed to fit.

Pretty soon, we were led out of the hotel on to the set, which was located a few blocks away. Initially, the directors asked us if we wanted a ride but the night air was cool, and we told them we preferred to walk. The whole cast—everyone—treated us like we were these famous American actors. Grant and I felt like we were walking on air. The light switch lady came along with us, and the whole time was going on about her daughter-in-law and how much she would like a photo of the two of us together. I waved my hand in front of my face; she didn't deserve to take my picture.

Qixian felt eerily similar to Taigu in a lot of ways: the architecture, the quiet neon-lit shops, the old men pedaling by on bicycles. It felt like this parallel universe where everything was just a little brighter and a little cleaner. In the center of town was its very own drum tower, a towering beacon from which the imperial army used to sound drums when there were intruders to alert the townspeople to evacuate. The sun was setting early and the drum tower was silent, as if to signal just the opposite—a quiet invitation to stay.

The set of the movie was in the outdoor pavilion of an ornate red structure that looked like it had been one of the few structures spared from the sprawling destruction of the Cultural Revolution. As we approached, we could already see the blindingly bright lights that projected artificial daylight onto the set. The pavilion was full of people in long crowded rows. Gorgeous women with immaculate painted faces gave embarrassed smiles as I passed. Young boys and girls—volunteer interns—scooted around passing out water and dinner boxes to the actors. We walked all the way up to the front of the building, where the director was sitting with his back to us high atop a stool between two giant display monitors.

A man, whose job it was to simply announce "quiet on the set" silenced all of the actors. The assistant director started to introduce us to him, but without pausing to turn around, the director simply raised his hand, still staring intently at the monitors. On them was the scene being shot inside the building—a KMT official was standing over the tortured and bloodied body of a Communist guard who had his arms tied behind a wooden chair. The official walked over to the guard and gave him a swift, hard punch across the face, shouting epithets and demanding to be told new information. The shadow across the tortured man's face was perfectly lit. The director nodded his head in approval and called scene.

His eyes turned to meet ours. I was surprised to find that he wasn't anything like I expected. He was a leathery old man, his face like a wax mannequin. His chin pooled into a blob at the base of his neck, and his hair was mottled and ratty and came to a ponytail at the back of his big head. Still, Grant and I knew what was at stake and needed desperately to impress him. He turned slowly in his chair and extended a meaty palm down to each of us.

"Where are you from?" he asked, looking at Grant, a question that was meant to stand in for our names.

"America," he answered proudly.

"And you?" the director questioned, pointing a long finger at me.

"Also America," I said, trying hard to match Grant's tone.

The director paused for a moment, taking stock of the two would-be actors. He removed a cigarette from a box atop the monitors and placed it to his lips.

"So your hair is dyed then?" he asked somewhat abruptly.

I scrunched up my face, not sure if I understood the question correctly. I didn't recognize the word "dye," so I stole a glance at Grant and he mouthed the word in English to me under his breath.

"No," I said. "This is my natural color." I knew that it was a mistake the moment I said it.

The director, lighting the cigarette, looked taken aback.

"Impossible," he said. "How can you Americans have black hair like us?"

"My mother is Chinese," I said, digging myself deeper.

"Chinese?" He sounded patently exasperated, like he had just been cheated in a game of mahjong. "Then how can you say that you're American?"

Everyone had gotten quiet all of the sudden, and they were staring at me like I was some strange, hideous being from another planet.

"I was born in America," I said slowly. "I'm an American."

The director shook his head. "Americans have blond hair, everyone knows that." He looked around the pavilion and members of the cast vigorously nodded their heads up and down in unison. He turned back to face me again.

"Would you consider dying it?"

My eyes grew wide. I had always held to my natural color; more than that, I'd never had the desire to change it.

"Maybe," I said, anxious to make concessions. The director's eyebrows were large and looming. "But it wouldn't look good," I said, trying hard to sound reasonable.

The director shook his head and cast a long look sidelong.

"How about you," he said, focusing his energy back on Grant. "Would you dye yours?"

Grant had light brown hair that parted neatly in the center. I saw immediately what the director was doing but I was too slow to do anything to stop it.

"Sure, I can dye it," Grant said, oblivious as always.

"Great," the director said. "Come back next week and we'll start filming your scenes." Grant found it necessary in that moment to clasp his hands together and bow, though nothing about Chinese society ever called for that. The assistant director motioned for us to follow him and the set retreated from view, the actors sitting with their noses turned up and the director's large menacing back turning to face us.

When we reached the hotel, the assistant director thanked us for coming and told Grant that he would be in touch with him about the following week. The light switch lady and the two of us piled into the same van and made the drive back to Taigu. The whole time I was sitting on the edge of my chair, like it was only a matter of time before a bomb would explode in my own chest. I had been that foolish American spy, believing the whole time that I actually stood a chance, when in reality I was just being used and deluded until I was no longer needed. When all was said and done, no other criteria seemed relevant.

Grant did his best to comfort me on the ride back, but I wasn't having it. I didn't doubt that he meant it, but it still came off as disingenuous. The light switch lady was up front making small talk with the driver that could almost have been called flirtatious. I sat back in my chair and tugged loosely at the hair on my head. The issue had come up before: regardless if I wanted to be Chinese or American, I would never be authentic enough.

When we got dropped off at the campus gates, the light switch lady went back to the girl's dormitory, and Grant and I ambled down the slanted path back to our house. When we rounded the bend from the main road, we heard a clamor surrounding Nate and Rachel's house. In that moment, I suddenly imagined that the film crew had commissioned a second shoot right on campus. I could see someone from the company having gone to see Rachel and Nate, thinking of two new parts for which they would be perfect. I felt this nagging jealousy well up inside of me, and broke into a sprint.

Had the events that unfolded been shot as a movie, the lighting would have been better and the music would have swelled dramatically in the background. In a pitch of rage, and with Grant running behind me, I stormed through their front door, pushing and shoving people aside. Suddenly, everything was quiet. This was the scene: a gaggle of young men dressed in blue smocks and wearing white facemasks were gathered around Rachel's bed. In between them, a white mess of red-splotched fur lay unmoving in a carrier, enveloped by heating pads and wrapped in a scarf. Initially, the doctors had deemed the surgery a success and sent Mumu back home. Not three hours later, her temperature dropped dramatically and the graduate students were left unsure what to do to save her life.

"Where were you?" Rachel cried frantically at the sight of me. "I was calling your phone all day."

I suddenly remembered my phone, which I had switched to silent ever since we left to go to Qixian. I turned to look at Grant—expecting blithe indifference—but instead, his face was as pained and shocked as mine, and for the first time, I saw myself reflected in him.

"Where *were* you?" she asked again, incredulously, her voice piercing the surrounding silence.

"I was…" I began, but my voice trailed off. The entire room was still. The camera did a slow zoom on Rachel's face—the bloodshot eyes, the clenched jaw. It panned down to show her hunched shoulders, the arms stretched weakly out in front of her.

I wanted nothing more than to tell her about what happened in Qixian—how unfair and wrong everything had been—but the words felt distant and out of place.

DESPAIR

After the big trip you may return to work feeling much better, but you'll probably find that things didn't get better after all. Nothing has changed. Nothing is happening. You may find an urge to close yourself in your room and read all the Western novels you never had a chance to before. You may find yourself giving vent to intense frustration in strange ways: cursing people in the market, breaking things in the kitchen, and so on.

Now is the time to push yourself. What may be hard to understand is that you are making progress. You are getting a feel for the culture, your job, how things work. You can push yourself by working hard at language and capitalizing on the few friendships you've begun to make. Avoid the temptation to travel away from your site. Stay with it! What may be causing you so much pain now has to do with your self-development.

This is the time when you can really invest yourself in the rest of your sojourn in Asia. It is also a time for you to come to grips with what within yourself is American and how much of that is important to you. You will have to draw some limits in your accommodation to another culture.

THE FLU

For two months, we could scarcely leave our own homes. Our lives were confined to the classrooms where we continued to teach, the tiny mess hall where we took our meals, and our red brick flats where we lived two to a house. We had all hoped it would be this temporary thing, a precautionary measure to ensure our safety. But the precise moment when the whole affair escalated from concern into crisis was impossible to pinpoint. The same was true of the point in time when we willingly acquiesced our American need for autonomy in favor of harmonious submission to the state.

By early autumn, swine flu had intensified into a global epidemic. Nearly every day, Grant forwarded us *New York Times* articles from his parents over the Great Firewall detailing the conditions back home. In China, there seemed to be a divide: in the South, due largely to a warmer climate, the situation was reported to be under control, but in the North, it was making daily headlines. The articles described the situation like it was happening in this faraway *other* place, but for us, it was home. "The cold is wearing down people's defenses, leaving them more at risk of becoming infected," the *Times* reported. "Two were found dead at Peking University in Beijing and many more are dropping off in the countryside every day."

In October, two students at Shanxi Agricultural University were rushed to the hospital under suspicion of carrying the virus. For days after, there was almost no information at all, and then, suddenly, like reception returning to a radio tower, it was all people could talk about. The dormitory where the students lived was quarantined and the rest of the school was put under lock-down. The walled campus complex, complete with barbed wire, became our own version of Alcatraz. No students were allowed to enter or exit any of the gates on campus. We were all trapped inside.

It was said to be an over-reactive response to what the media described as a failed handling of the SARS epidemic back in 2003. Then, the Chinese government didn't acknowledge the gravity of the virus until its citizens had already boarded planes and carried the disease to places far and wide. I heard harrowing stories of the Fellows living in China at the time—how they had to be emergency airlifted back to the states for four months before the situation settled down, and how they could only then return to their teaching posts. But I never thought it would happen to me.

The decree came from Xiao Yin, our main boss in the Foreign Affairs Office. At the time, we were all too overwhelmed to say anything. The office organized our lives and in turn we were expected to follow our contractual obligations to the letter. They told us that we would be held to the same restrictions as the students at the university, but they did allow one concession: we were permitted to go off-campus so long as we got clearance from the office, though we couldn't go further than the town limits. We were almost certainly granted this privilege because we were foreigners; even the veteran Chinese teachers at the school didn't have the same right.

The first night that we got word of the new regulations, I had planned to go out to karaoke with some of my grad students and the other teachers in town. As we were getting ready to leave, the main entrance to the school was a mass of pitched bodies, confused and angry as to why they couldn't get out. The guards seemed equally bewildered, unsure of how to deal with the mob, short of simply locking them behind an iron gate. In a stroke of spur-of-the-moment thinking, we were able to frame my students as our translators and make it safely outside. But after that first day of pandemonium, the administration got wise, and that was the last time my students, or any students, saw daylight outside of campus.

Within days, other freedoms started to disappear. There was a 10:00 PM curfew instated; students were expected to return to their dormitories and lights out was set at 11:00. Another dormitory was quarantined and the whole place was partitioned off like a giant construction site. I remember the tall cranes that blanketed the building in fine mesh netting before wrapping it in plastic. Bio-hazard crews dressed in hazmat suits had to deliver pre-packaged food and water to students in those rooms three times a day. They had disaster relief trucks parked outside.

There were only three reasons why we ever left the school. The first was for variety in our diet. About once a week, the office conceded to our desire for a meal out at one of the hot pot or buffet restaurants in town. The second was to stock up on groceries and other essentials at *Jia Jia Li* that weren't available at the campus supermarket. These included most non-packaged goods—eggs, yogurt, meat, and fresh produce. The third was leaving for the sake of leaving. We reveled in our temporary freedom—like inmates let out for an hour of daily exercise.

A team of camo-clad security guards monitored the flow of traffic in and out of the gates at every entrance to the school. Each was armed with a black, handheld device that more resembled a speed detector more than it did a thermometer. All of us were required to carry our "Foreign Expert Certificates" every time we wanted to leave campus, even though our faces would have been proof enough of our status as non-students. We could often leave campus without much difficulty, but the return trip would always end with a speed gun to the head to make sure we were still well enough not to infect the ten thousand students made completely vulnerable by being restricted on campus.

By then it was already early November, and Taigu saw the first big snowfall of the year. All teachers and students were required to take their temperature readings twice a day, at 7:30 and 11:00 AM, and had to report to the authorities if their readings were in any way abnormal. High temperatures often signified nothing more than a seasonal cold, but because of the looming fear of indefinite hospitalization—standard practice at the time—students became more and more wary of revealing that they were sick, even to their peers. It was like something out of the McCarthy hearings—the school's administration counted on students to turn in their friends for the sake of the community's wellness.

It all felt like a war zone; within the closed gates there was an almost visceral feeling of desolation. Even those who lived nearby couldn't go home, and loved ones had to greet sons and daughters at the main gate to deliver food and other care packages. The students were even more ignorant of the details of the situation than we were, since many did not own computers or have access to the news on TV. The school gave us their reasons, but we still couldn't help feeling like the victims of some shadowy conspiracy. The entire student body, like us, was left with an overwhelming sense of powerlessness; we had no real defense against catching the disease, and with the school locked down, we couldn't do much else but sit around and wait for the whole mess to blow over.

I was made increasingly aware every day that I was living in China. It was hard to imagine that anything on this scale could ever happen in the states—there would be intense pressure on local and state governments to improve the situation, and, almost certainly, riots. I was surprised to the degree that everyone seemed to know and accept their roles and play them without any outward objection. Here, push-back manifested itself in subtler ways; not every rule was as ironclad as the administration wanted to believe.

At the far east side of campus there were no gates, only a brick-and-mortar wall. The ground was sloped and uneven, probably compacted with excess earth from when the indoor pool was excavated. There were no academic buildings, and the fields were littered with heaps of garbage and unused building materials. Almost nobody ever traipsed out that far, but when the campus got locked down, word quickly spread. Without guards, and with a patch of space where the upward-sloping ground met a lower-lying part of the wall, students could flee the coop. They could boost one another up over the top and hoist each other down over the barbed wire to the other side. The same worked in reverse. Taxis and unlicensed black cabs even started to idle on the side of the street, never knowing when the next crop of passengers would emerge.

The administration began selectively deciding which institutions on campus would be shut down and which would continue to operate. More than anything, it drew attention to the hypocritical measures that the university took to prevent the transfer of disease. Whereas the large indoor pool facility was deemed too conducive to germ-spreading, the neighboring bathhouse, which had to absorb all those needy shower-goers, was given the green light. All classes of 50 or more students were canceled, but student dorms for undergraduates routinely saw eight students crammed to a single room. Even in the midst of hysteria, we were still expected to teach our 35-student classes as if nothing had changed.

The biggest setback was the loss of North Yard. With none of the students able to leave the campus gates, all of the neighboring and outlying businesses began to go under. At first, the school simply locked the gate. Then, when they realized that students could still use the gaps in the grating to climb over it, they filled them in with bricks. After a wall of bricks adjacent to the gate still wasn't adequate, they posted a guard there to watch for escapees. Only when it was clear that no more students were leaving campus, did fruit sellers, vendors, and shop owners pack up and leave town—relegating themselves to finding new work, and abandoning the district to quiet desertion. No restaurant better exemplified this than Manhattan's.

It was easy to write the place off. Manhattan's looked just as crummy as any other shop in North Yard—a buckling sheet-metal shack in a long line of restaurants. In the days when it was still operational, it was run out of this grungy, dimly-lit vault that looked like a condemned crime scene. There was a sliding glass door on the outside with a bike lock looped around its solid metal handlebars. That was how it stayed for months after it closed, a tiny placard taped to the glass announcing that it had gone out of business and that the space was available for rent.

Nate introduced us to the restaurant during my first year. He told us that there was this Western fast food joint with actual chicken burgers in North Yard. We were immediately sold. I couldn't explain it at the time, but I could trick myself when I ate there. By then, we had already started to tire of the noodles and oily vegetables that were staples of northern Chinese cooking. It wasn't that they were bad—the food was one of the best things about the town—but even the braised eggplant with its pockets of gooey redness got to be so routine that it became almost sickening to look at. There was never a ton of variety in the cuisine as it was, and anything *not* Chinese was rare, almost out of the question.

Not one month had passed before I began to feel intense, almost violent cravings for Western food. Things that I would have turned my nose at in America suddenly became wildly desirable—beef hamburgers, chicken tenders, warm fries, milkshakes. Even something as simple as instant coffee made my eyes bulge. I felt I had betrayed my former self, the idealist in me, who for so long had stubbornly refused to eat fast food. On long road trips in the states, my friends used to roll their eyes and groan. Now I was seeking out this filth with vehement conviction. I tried to rationalize it, too—blame it on some innate cultural allegiance—but the truth was undeniable: I just needed a burger.

The first thing you noticed about Manhattan's was the silver tinsel Christmas tree propped up in the far corner. It was out there for so long that even the fake branches were wilting. The silver had rubbed off, and all that was left was sharp, brassy fuzz that looked like it might come alive and attack at any moment. There were giant mirrors that covered the walls and a scratchy black-and-white TV that seemed to only play old episodes of *America's Funniest Home Videos* on loop. There was no audio, so we had to imagine the studio laugh track for ourselves. Every time we came in, there was another man on skis colliding with a snow bank or a father being jabbed in the balls by his son.

The inside of Manhattan's was furnished with blue fluorescent lights that hung in deep concave shades like the hair dryers in old beauty salons. In the evening, after the sun set, the lights cast threatening shadows across the tables and chairs, all of which were made out of that awful hard-molded green and orange plastic that you see in washed-up, 50s-era diners. The glass display case on the counter was always empty and there was never more than one menu to share. But enough daylight used to come in during the afternoon that it wasn't entirely unpleasant, and that was when the few of us used to go.

At our height, we were going twice a week—usually on the weekends during lunch. There was something about the place that kept us coming back. The boss who ran it was as sweet as they come. He was a slight man of at least 50, soft-spoken with this great lilt to his voice; no request we made was ever too outlandish. There was no other staff, so he did everything himself. He didn't look like your typical restaurant manager, and I always felt like he had been goaded into opening the place to begin with, that there was the promise of a franchise that never panned out, but he had already bought the deep fryer and the burger flipper and needed to put them to good use.

He always gave us discounts for being good customers. He made these special laminated VIP cards to use and earn points for future purchases, but the cards didn't have room for punches or stamps, and it didn't matter whether we brought them or not. To his credit, the fries were always piping hot, and they had real American ketchup (McCormick). It was rare to see other customers, which helped explain why they eventually went under, but that meant never having to wait in line. We could just about own the place, plant a flag in the middle of the table and claim it for America. In all the times I went, I only ever saw one other person—a heavyset, balding man—parked at the green table right in front of the TV.

On our first trip we all got chicken burgers. They had these gorgeous pictures of double-decker patties with seeded buns that looked like they were from the states. I knew in my heart that they were fake—not a single restaurant in the world ever has accurate pictures. Beyond that, half of the other items they advertised in the store window were not even on the menu. Biting into the burger was like piercing a wet dishrag that reeked of livestock. I didn't even know if it was meat; I don't remember if I finished it.

It should not have come as a shock that Manhattan's closed—no fast food place had ever managed to make it in Taigu. Nate told us about a pizza shop in North Yard during his first year that was run by a young couple who brewed coffee using what looked like stolen chemistry equipment. They made pizzas in an easy bake oven. By the time the spring semester started, they were gone. Then there was

Popland's, which sold chicken sandwiches that trumped Manhattan's in terms of quality. But it was far away—well past *Jia Jia Li* and near the county limits—and we went there about as often as we did to the McDonald's in Taiyuan for their syrupy egg sandwiches and big breakfast combos. Manhattan's was the closest thing to home.

By the time it did close, the number of nearby restaurants was limited literally to the handful that were located *on*-campus as opposed to *off*. As a result, the underground supermarket and the cafeterias quickly pushed capacity to accommodate for the lack of other dining options. We ate almost exclusively at the little mess hall where Rui Wan, the cook hired for us by the Foreign Affairs Office, made dinners and some weekend meals in addition to our usual lunches at times when she had previously had off.

Almost everything came to be categorized in this *on/off* divide. I had a conspiracist notion that the whole lock-down was devised by the school to create a monopoly over the student market. Nearly all of the other businesses were squeezed out and students had nowhere else to go. Naturally, the school began price gouging. Each of the campus-affiliated institutions were easily making three or four times the profit they were making prior to the crisis.

When Manhattan's was finally sold and reopened a few months later, the new owners converted the entire restaurant into a goat soup place. I remember the first day we saw it. One of our Chinese friends brought us over and it was hard to wrap my head around the fact that Manhattan's was really gone. The soup was made using ground-up bits of intestine and goat stomach. Its name had the character 杂 in it that is also part of the Chinese word for complicated. While we were waiting for our bowls, I asked one of the waitresses if she knew what happened to Manhattan's. Her face contorted like she had just been splashed with hot oil.

"We don't serve that kind of food," she said, with a grimace. No one really knew how the new place fared after that; we weren't all that interested in goat stew.

Later, when we reminisced about Manhattan's, in the same beleaguered breath that we mentioned the all-you-can-eat barbecue place that had also shut its doors, our stories were always slightly different. It was still during the swine flu fiasco, and we were at Jerry and Darren's house during one of our Thursday "Open Mic" Nights. Paired with a home-cooked meal every Thursday, they were just about all we had left. Outside of teaching, there wasn't much for us to do. With the pool closed and snow blanketing the basketball courts and track fields, exercise became untenable. Moderately large gatherings of any kind were forbidden, which meant that dance parties and German nights went the way of Manhattan's and the rest of the businesses in North Yard.

For almost all other occasions, I spent the majority of my time at Nate and Rachel's house. It felt nice to commiserate, to have the assurance that there were people who were going through the exact same thing as I was. It made the whole experience feel less lonely. Still, after a while, their four ashen walls came to represent the boundaries of my own existence. I wished we could have all taken just one more trip to Walmart in Taiyuan before it no longer was an option.

The mic stand was still up at Jerry and Darren's and the computer was plugged into the AUX jack on the speakers. Jerry's electric guitar lay on a mound of jackets near the door. Earlier, one of Jerry's students had performed "I Want It That Way" with a surprising command of the English lyrics. Darren told a dirty joke involving a misguided sailor and a field of magic mushrooms. Nate did an impromptu stand-up routine about how the off-brand Oreos in Taigu promoted diarrhea, and even though he'd done it before, we were all drunk enough by that point that we were howling with laughter. Bobby and Lynn had left, and with the rest of our Chinese friends gone, it was just the six Americans and Luca sitting around on the stained green-and-white couches looking for an excuse not to go home.

There was a box of Blue Lion in the center of the floor and we all took turns draining can after can of the stale-tasting beer. Darren started talking about the guy who used to own Manhattan's, and how during the first wave of the epidemic, the owner offered to pay him to take orders from students and deliver them over the wall because we were the only ones who could leave the gates. Grant started in about the blue lamps, how the whole place looked like a glorified truck stop. I said that it looked more like a hollowed out bomb-shelter to me, what might survive after a nuclear apocalypse. I remembered the clips of *America's Funniest Home Videos* playing non-stop on the TV and how scary it was that these small, sad, insignificant moments of real people might remain long after they were gone.

Then Rachel asked the question that no one wanted to answer: "If the food was so bad, why did we keep going back?" We all got pretty quiet. I kept looking at the dusty sill next to the bookshelf, the windows that had been sealed in plastic and then draped with thick curtains to keep the room warm.

Finally, Nate said something like: "I think I drank too much *baijiu* in those days to remember." We all laughed. He took out his wallet and showed us the VIP card he still kept flattened against the leather. Then he said: "It was one of Taigu's great losses." That's when we all nodded. I thought about every time I had ever eaten at Manhattan's, how there was a part of me that absolutely despised it—the rancid food, the goddamn tree, everything—and a part that left me transfixed and wanting more.

AT NIGHT

At night, we took walks around campus, careful to only hold hands in the dark places where we knew we wouldn't get caught. The main drag was off-limits, as was the spotlit area near the big track. So was "Lover's Forest," where too many of our students came to steal precious moments of pseudo-privacy in the tree-lined pavilion. Shining a flashlight at night, there was always a danger of coming face-to-face with one of these couples, leaned up against a tree or hunkered down on the hard stone benches. My heart jumped every time I skimmed over something moving in the pitch black, but I quickly learned to avert my gaze. The couples had to redouble their efforts because of the cold, brushing away ice and sitting statuesque, carrying on as no more than silhouettes of insulated jackets.

We started by the cluster of foreign houses and made a big loop, crossing over the narrow hexagonal paths, through the monolith of student dorms and up past the pool. Sometimes Rachel and I would take a different route back, curving around the West Gate and through the rows of fields and greenhouses reserved for agricultural experiments. Like the other foreign teachers, we had our own homes, so we didn't need the outdoor privacy in the same way that our students did, but we did need to get out. Rachel was particularly adamant. She was less Chinese than I was but she would always cite these proverbs her students told her about needing to digest properly and how walking after dinner was good for *qi* flow. People always lauded how adjusted she was, how assimilated to the culture.

A big freeze followed the snowstorm that hit Taigu shortly after Halloween. Snow was cleared from the major streets, but all of the smaller paths were still glazed over with a thick sheet of ice, which had built up from compacted snow and temperatures that were routinely below freezing. For a while, we all treated the snowfall like it was some miraculous gift—like someone had taken pity on us. In need of some kind of respite from the suffocating swine flu restrictions imposed by the college, we found our savior in fluffy clumps of water vapor falling from the sky. Snow provided us the chance to fill our otherwise monotonous weekends with an outdoor activity that could still be enjoyed within the safe confines of the university walls.

Soon, winter cheer sprang up everywhere on campus. The two outdoor tracks and the basketball courts were filled with meticulously crafted snow sculptures. One Saturday, I took photos around campus with a small group of my students. We paused at what must have been every "scenic spot"—old buildings, the university's ornate gates—every time trying to one-up our previous pose. Rachel and Lynn made hot chocolate in the afternoons, using some of the stock chocolate available at the supermarket, paired with a generous helping of cocoa powder brought over from the states. Rachel even constructed a snowman in front of her house, using anise stars for the eyes, twigs for the eyebrows, a sun hat and bandanna as accoutrements, and a cigarette poking out of its mouth.

In class, we became the teachers we had all wished we had growing up. The foreigners all played tricks on each other, ambushing classes with armfuls of snowballs aimed squarely at the front podium. With twenty minutes to spare at the end of one class, I marched outside with an entire group of thirty graduate students, and proceeded to have a snowball fight. In the first moments, everyone was hesitant, and it took the raucous young hot shot, Alva, to throw the first snowball at his teacher. But once that was done, there was no stopping my other students. I walked home from class that day, my shoes more than a bit soppy and my blazer in dire need of a trip to the dry cleaners, but with a lightness I hadn't had in weeks.

That was all before we heard the news. The snow that year didn't stop with the initial ten inches. Over the next few days, Taigu saw quite a bit more—sheets of white that covered tree boughs and blanketed narrow stone walkways. Authorities and civilians throughout Northern China were astonished at the swiftness and intensity of the snowfall. It was a record amount for the region, the biggest snowstorm since 1955. We turned a deaf ear to the reported casualties, of people trapped in their homes, of the cars stranded from Beijing to Shijiazhuang. People were using blunt household objects to clear the snow—rakes, dustpans, brooms. No one was prepared for the onslaught. When the snow melted, so too did our hopes of leaving campus. With the ground cleared, it was easy to remember exactly where we were standing.

It got dark early at night, and the air was so thick that we could feel it sticking to the backs of our throats like stale taffy. For months, the campus was masked in that perpetual haze, veiling everything as blunted outlines and shapes. We speculated that part of it was from winter fog, but we attributed a lot to the coal dust that billowed out of Shanxi's famously abundant factories and went toward powering our heat and electricity. It was strange to live in a place where pollution was both ubiquitous and normalized. If it wasn't from burning coal, it was almost certainly from burning trash—one of the most popular forms of waste management. The smell was almost palpable at times, and burning paper, compost, and plastic peppered the air with black streaks.

The roads outside were still too icy to take runs on without fear of slipping, but the school opened the pool again after a time, so after class, Rachel, Grant, Nate and I all went. Grant was on the swim team at Oberlin and rarely said a word the whole time he swam. Nate was a great sprinter and Rachel's family lived near the ocean for most of her life. I was hands-down the weakest swimmer among the teachers, but like most things about Taigu, there wasn't a whole lot of competition. The students were militant about doing physical activity in the cold; any time outside of walking to class was spent in their dorms. As a result, we had the pool nearly all to ourselves. The water was frigid, and I got used to swimming faster and longer than I ever had before. By December I was pulling in close to a mile a day—enjoying the silent, almost meditative quality to the repetition of the strokes.

Without exception, every one of the restaurants on campus had closed—a combination of the swine flu scare and the snowfall killing off too much business. After swimming, we had dinner at 6:00 at the makeshift cafeteria by the Foreign Affairs Office. Rui Wan kept a modest two-burner stove in the back where all of the surfaces were glazed with a layer of dried grease. She always served rice porridge (*zhou*), which she told us was good to stay warm during the winter, and paired it with a single doughy *baozi*. Jerry rarely ate his *zhou*, so I usually had a second bowl to myself. Sometimes there would be strips of cabbage in vinegar or another vegetable for the few of us to share. The porridge went right through me after the meals. It felt like a prisoner's diet. Between the exercise and the food, I must have lost ten pounds that winter.

We all coped with the situation in our own ways. There were the times we saw each other during the day, and then there were all those other times that weren't accounted for, when we didn't know what the others were up to. We came to spend so much time together that any time apart felt unsettling, like we were all halves of people unable to function properly on our own. Monday was German night, Tuesday was TV night, and every Thursday Jerry invited us over to drink beer and mess around with his audio equipment. It was strange to think about Jerry or Darren or Nate alone in their houses, or even of Grant in the room next door to mine with the door closed and the shades drawn. Everyone coped in different ways. But Rachel and I had each other.

Sometimes after dinner, we walked to the underground supermarket on campus. At that point, it had become the social hub for the entire student body, since the university had already closed most other indoor gathering locales. In addition to being a fairly comprehensive supermarket, the underground was also home to an athletics store, two cellphone offices, a bookstore, and a number of smaller vendor stands selling everything from MP3 players to school stationery. We came to make almost daily trips ourselves, stocking up on yogurt and snacks for lack of more meaningful activities.

There were a few tables that were always jammed with students playing cards, chain-smoking, and spitting seed shells all over the floor. Its main draw was the warmth and its being slightly less cramped than the student dormitories. It was the only place on campus that still felt somehow *living,* like there were live people who we could go up to and interact with if we so chose. The grocery shelves looked like bandits had rifled through them. The school couldn't provide enough food to keep up with student demand, and goods were perpetually out of stock. It could have been a scene out of the Great Leap Forward, of the famines that devastated China under Mao, when no one was given enough to eat and each family had meal tickets that they could trade in for monthly rations.

It was at the supermarket where it first became clear that Nate was depressed. He paced the aisles, picking up the stray case of beer or bottle of *baijiu* that he would neglect to mention and we would never see turn up at parties. At home, he played video games in the afternoon until Grant or I dragged him out of the house to go swimming, and then, after dinner, he was back on it again for the rest of the night.

"If they don't let us go to Shanghai," he used to say, "I don't know what I'm going to do."

He started to cancel his classes increasingly more regularly. We got our flu shots, but we still didn't know if our bosses would let us leave for Thanksgiving. We should have done more at the time, but we were oblivious to Nate like we were to everything else. We were all too preoccupied with ourselves.

After we left the supermarket, we almost always made a stop at a copy shop. My favorite one was a little mom-and-pop stand not too far from the main teaching building. It was the only one open past 10:00 PM, and we got used to spending a portion of our evenings shoving papers and USB sticks through the crowds of students to get our teaching materials prepared. The entire family operated out of this tiny 90 square-foot storefront. In the mornings, the dad played Warcraft or watched Chinese dramas on the computer as the daughter helped customers. By the afternoon, the mom was there while her newborn slept on a blanket in a makeshift crib of old copy paper boxes. In the evenings, the four of them ate dinner, sometimes with their son-in-law, scooping out rice and fatty bits of pork with cup measures from a communal steamer.

Rachel dropped my hand every time we rounded the corner to the shop. Aside from the foreigners and Bobby and Lynn, all anyone else could do was speculate about our relationship. We were careful never to show any outward feelings in the presence of others, something that I wasn't used to. But that wasn't so strange, considering my life in this new place and my relationships with everyone being changed by the experience. That was the way Rachel preferred it, and I deferred to her judgment because she was my Senior Fellow and she had lived here for a year longer than I.

Still, it gnawed at me, the feeling that what we were doing needed to be kept a secret because it was wrong or because she was in some way ashamed of it. She told me a lot about Bart, one of the foreign teachers at the university in her first year; how they would get drunk and have sex and the next day pretend like nothing had happened. He was a big guy, she said, and not particularly her type.

I suspected that she was jaded in the same way we would all be—how this place had forced us to draw from our own small community or else deal with being alone. There were no other foreigners, and students and locals were essentially off-limits. Taigu was strange in that way—you ended up getting involved with people you wouldn't expect. But with me, she said, things were different. I hazarded to agree. The conditions weren't perfect but they could have been worse. We had already broken the first rule of the fellowship. No one was supposed to fall in love.

We kept a low profile whenever we passed the "Keepers of the Square" practicing Crazy English out behind the abandoned bus depot. They were a zealous cult of students who used a method of rote shouting to improve their English ability. We were never sure about the effectiveness of their practice, but they still garnered a considerable crowd night after night. Rachel told me that early on in her first year she was curious about all the yelling and was goaded into leading one of the dialogues. She described the whole ordeal as terrifying, having been the possessor of this fluency that everyone there was trying to attain. It helped then that we could pass as Chinese—if we bundled our scarves over our noses and mouths, we almost blended in.

At home, we tried to ignore the scurrying sounds of the rats inside the walls and above our ceiling tiles. Rachel and Nate had two cats at their house so it wasn't as much of an issue, but Grant was allergic and the Foreign Affairs Office didn't have any other ideas for how to deal with the problem. The incessant squeaking kept me awake at night until we started doing something about it. It wasn't uncommon to find one in the morning, half-stuck to the side of a glue trap, and do the nasty deed of disposal. Eventually, Grant got so comfortable that he would catch rats in a live trap and drown them himself in a bucket in his bathroom. It was like the cold had sapped our empathic response; we could hardly feel anything anymore.

With the shades drawn and the lights dim, we made steaming cups of hot water and sneaked lopsidedly into bed. Rachel and I talked about our lesson plans for the next day, how after all these months she still got nervous getting up to the podium and saying those first few words at the start of every class. She rolled over to her side and joked about something that Nate had said at lunch, or how cold the pool was that day, or when the next time Rui Wan would make *jiaozi* for dinner. If there had been a world outside the campus walls, we were scarcely aware of its existence. She held my hand again like she had in the shadows. We shut off the lights and in the dull glow of the moonlight, we imagined the front gates open, the cool wind streaming through its metal bars.

IF THERE IS
NO ALCOHOL,
YOU CAN'T
SAY ANYTHING

I was sitting across the table from Xiao Yin, both of us dressed in suit jackets and ties, and each holding a shot of *baijiu* raised expectantly towards the ceiling. We were on the first of three mandatory, pre-dinner shots. The appetizers were being presented on the giant, self-revolving Lazy Susan, and Xiao Yin had just started telling us the story of how he had applied to become a member of the Communist Party.

"In my time it wasn't as competitive as it is now," he said in Chinese. Only during banquets did I ever hear him speak Mandarin; none of the other Chinese officials were as fluent as he was in English. When he was just with us foreign teachers, he insisted on speaking English. I imagined it was an old habit—something he picked up from overseeing the first group of foreign teachers for which he was responsible in the late 1980s, when he started working in the Foreign Affairs Office.

"Now there are all these rules and regulations—written tests, interviews, background checks." He took a glance around the table. "If this were the case then, I would probably not be here today!" Polite laughter rippled across the room. All seven of the foreign teachers were seated on the right half of the large circular table. Two university professors, three of our bosses—Li Feng, Zhao Huang, and Hao He—and Party Secretary Gao, the evening's guest of honor, sat on the left.

"But, that is not the case for this man," Xiao Yin said, extending his hand to the man seated to his right at the center of the table. "Party Secretary Gao has been a capable and loyal member of the party ever since he climbed the ranks and took over here at Shanxi Agricultural University in 2001. Knowing that many of you will be leaving Taigu soon, he has been kind enough to grace us with his presence."

We all gave a round of applause as Party Secretary Gao stood up quickly to be thanked. It was nearing the end of my first year, and Rachel, Nate, Darren, and Luca would all be leaving the university in a few weeks. The school organized banquets for special occasions and this one was to be the senior teachers' final send-off.

"So I would like to first propose a toast to him," Xiao Yin said finally. "*Ganbei!*" We all tapped our tiny shot glasses politely at the edge of the Lazy Susan and knocked back the *baijiu* to the farthest reaches our throats would allow. The party secretary was a thin, slight man with hair slicked back like Elvis. His wrinkles sloped down the front of his forehead like a terraced rice field. I had seen him on campus once or twice prior, but primarily we maintained a distance from school officials who really had no bearing on our day-to-day lives and who had little idea of the specifics of what we did or why we were even at the school.

Banquets involved a lot of eating, drinking, and networking in the midst of drunken antics. No one really knew the other people there all that well, but everyone got dressed up to sit in a fancy room with many more courses of food than there were people at the table, all ballyhooing and having a good time. For us, it usually meant making small talk, getting thanked for whatever contributions Party bigwigs could improvise on the spot, and spending the rest of the time exuberantly toasting. Knocking back drinks was supposed to, it seemed, flesh out a relationship that didn't really exist; it was the alcohol that bonded us more than anything else.

"Second," he said, I would also like to offer a toast to four teachers who will not be coming back next year." He signaled the four of them to stand up. "Thank you for all of your work to this school and best of luck in the future."

We were all seated around the large circular table, arranged in descending importance, relative to the party secretary. Xiao Yin took it upon himself to personally place us in order.

Between the two of us, Grant had historically gotten top billing. This was largely because his Chinese was so much better than mine when we first arrived and that Xiao Yin took an immediate liking to his gregarious banter with the other cadres. At first, I was jealous of Grant—the fact that he had been singled out and was doted upon by our head boss—but gradually I came to appreciate my position at the lower end of the table. There was no expectation of me to make futile conversation with any of the officials or have the burden of taking drinks for Xiao Yin if he got sick and refused. So Grant was seated to the left of our boss, and I was left somewhere in the middle.

Next to Grant was Rachel, whom Xiao Yin took to calling "queen" on account of her being the only female foreign teacher. Then it was Nate, my other Senior Fellow, and then any combination of Darren, Jerry, and I filled in the next three positions. With even less of a formal relationship, Luca, the German teacher, was almost always seated last.

There was a part of me that really looked forward to the banquets, and another part that chafed at the phenomenal waste of energy and productivity. The resulting drunken stupor made us useless for the rest of the day. Almost without fail at the end of each banquet, we ended up staggering back home, either ready to continue the drunken revelry or pass out from exhaustion. But more often than not, despite the claims that alcohol would actually make us "teach better," we felt so sick after especially insipid lunch banquets that we had to cancel afternoon class.

"Finally," Xiao Yin concluded, "I want to thank our three teachers who will be returning next year. We look forward to having another year with you." Again we all raised our glasses, clapped them down on the Lazy Susan, and shot them back. Never in my professional life had I envisioned having the opportunity to get drunk with my boss, and in Taigu, it was less an invitation than an outright obligation.

An aversion to alcohol or a refusal to drink came with an incredible loss of face for the host—in this case, our bosses at the Foreign Affairs Office and the high-powered school and Communist officials who we dined with—so, the best way to show our respect and gratitude was to drink, and drink a lot. Like most things in China, there was a culture and etiquette to drinking. There was a method for whom to toast first and when, as well as how often.

The waitresses started bringing over the main dishes in courses. The best part about banquets was getting to eat, for free, endless amounts of exquisite food that we would normally never buy on our own. The Lazy Susan spun first a plate of sweet-and-sour shrimp, a spit of fried braised lamb dangling from between two skillets, and a small plate of abalone. I was careful never to be the first one to cut into any of the dishes, letting the large glass plate spin until each dish reached Party Secretary Gao and then continued languidly down the line.

After the initial three toasts, the rules loosened for subsequent drinks. Either you got up and toasted someone else or they got up and toasted you. Occasionally you could make another big toast at the center of the table for everyone to drink, but mostly people split it up. I made it my secret mission to toast the guest of honor before any of the other foreigners—my own form of brown-nosing. After the dishes had circulated a few rotations and I had taken a couple of swipes of each one with my chopsticks, I decided to take the first crack at the head of the table.

"Mr. Gao," I said, the glass tipped and outstretched in my hands. "Thank you for your care in watching over us and for your constant help." I could have basically spewed off any nicety that fit that basic structure.

"Yes, thank you," Party Secretary Gao replied, and after a moment added, "for all that you do." We clinked glasses, mine edged down half the length of his—a sign of modesty and respect—and turned them over after we were done drinking to show that we had finished it all. As I turned to walk back to my seat, I snuck the requisite grimace from the *baijiu* that I was always careful to hide.

Following my lead, staff and professors began toasting with one another, and some came down over to our side to toast with us too. It was rude not to toast with someone if they occupied a higher social standing than you. High-level Communist officials, or *ganbu*, had to drink as part of their jobs, and, for the most part, if you couldn't drink, you didn't get ahead. A student of mine who was applying to become a Party member once told me that male members were expected to be able to drink an entire bottle of *baijiu* or a whole case of beer in a single sitting.

In truth, though, it wasn't only Communist officials who drank. There was a certain ease with which drinking cut across all sectors of the population in China. I remembered a lesson with Leslie where he went over a joke that had been circulating on the internet. It listed the reasons why different people drank and the role that alcohol played. "Without drinking," it said, "high-level cadres wouldn't have a friend. Without drinking, mid-level cadres wouldn't have any information. Without drinking, low-level cadres wouldn't have a shred of hope. Without drinking, disciplinary enforcers wouldn't have a clue. Without drinking, commoners wouldn't have any happiness. Without drinking, brothers wouldn't have any feeling. And without drinking, men and women wouldn't have a chance!"

At some point, the fourteen of us had finished all three urn-shaped bottles of *baijiu* and began moving on to beer. By that point in the meal, the alcohol was hitting hard and everyone was indiscriminately toasting with one another, doing away with all formality. I looked around the room. Nate and Darren were getting into it with one another, each trying to outdrink the other. Grant was still up at the front hobnobbing with Xiao Yin and the others. Rachel was already a beet red—she was even more allergic to alcohol than I was. Luca had a small collection of glass beer bottles at his feet, having a particular hatred of *baijiu* and not having any desire to be held in the good graces of any Party officials.

Drinking culture was logic-defying, and nothing more so than its best kept secret: no one actually liked to drink. *Baijiu* was notoriously caustic, and even Tsingtao, the most expensive and highly-touted domestic beer, tasted bland and watered-down. At banquets and big dinners, alcohol was a necessary evil, little more than a social lubricant. Aside from alcoholics, few people in China were casual drinkers—they either drank because they had to or they didn't. More accurately, people appreciated the powers that alcohol afforded them, the ability to loosen up and speak their minds without consequence. Being drunk absolved you of virtually all guilt; people tolerated behavior of all sorts without so much as a second thought.

With the once intricately presented dishes now eviscerated, Xiao Yin approached the table to make the final toast of the evening and to call for an end to the banquet. I had just made a rousing seven-way toast with all of the other foreign teachers celebrating the simple fact that we had made it through the year together. All of the alcohol filled me with a sort of boundless invincibility, so much so, that just as Xiao Yin was about to speak, I interrupted him.

"Wouldn't it be great if we had banquets all the time next year," I asked dumbly, the *baijiu* swirling around in my head.

I was half-expecting him to chastise me for trying to say something without a drink in my hand, but a sudden grief came over him instead. Xiao Yin's entire job called for constant wining and dining—making visiting scholars and new teachers feel welcome on campus. He managed a smile from underneath a down-turned scowl, the bags under his eyes deep-set and heavy.

"That would mean you'd have to drink every day," he said, his hair stiff and gray next to his slowly reddening face. "And you really wouldn't want that."

After the banquet dispersed, we stumbled our way towards Nate and Rachel's house, the site of most of our nighttime revelry. The scent of vinegar from the nearby processing plant was strong and pungent in the air and I breathed it in, thankful that it wasn't the rotting broccoli smell we were so used to at that time of night. Not feeling well, Grant opted to go to home early in spite of a chorus of jeers from the other foreigners. Nate and Luca mysteriously up and disappeared too, and so for a while it was just the four of us—Rachel, Darren, Jerry, and me—with the energy and maturity level of six-year-olds, letting loose in Rachel's living room.

Immediately we started rearranging the furniture, pushing the couches and loveseats over towards the far walls so that there was a space in the middle to dance. Jerry plugged his phone into the speaker jack and Darren went to the fridge to get more beer. Seizing an opportunity, I took Rachel by the shoulders and started swinging her around the room. I was stomping my feet to Jerry's techno music, and taking long galloping strides.

Grabbing on to me perhaps a bit too tightly, Rachel screamed over the music into my ear, "I just... I just want to go to bed." Her voice was raspy and she was slumped up against the wall. Usually quite tolerant of our shenanigans, this time the alcohol made her groggy and she looked like she could collapse into sleep at any moment. Her allergy gave rise to red spots that blossomed like hyacinth all over her body when she drank. It used to be a bit jarring to see her naked after she drank, like she was perpetually coming down with a new bout of chickenpox.

I relented, handing her the keys to my house. "You sleep first, I'll just meet you when things finish up here," I shouted, apparently unaware that I could simply lower the volume on the speaker instead. It seemed unnatural to have to kick everyone out and stop the revelry like that. *Better that she just go to bed,* I thought. She gave me a cutting glare that I mistook for tiredness and walked out through the door, slamming it hard when she left.

Shortly after Rachel was gone, I heard a loud banging on the door. At first it was just a single knock, but in the time it took for me to get to it, the solid wooden door was bouncing in its frame. When I opened it, I saw Nate and Luca squealing, almost at the point of bursting. They had their heads stacked sideways one on top of the other in the narrow opening like in those old Marx Brothers films, and told us to come outside.

Luca's guitar was lying strings up on the brick banister, and in that moment it looked a bit like a corpse, dressed in thin pinstripes, its hands like curved Cs at its side. Luca, with a face like a greedy child, held a stubby red firecracker in his hand. In addition to the fireworks, the two of them had bought another case of beer from the corner *xiaomaibu,* the only store open past 10:00 PM. Spring Festival was long over, but the mess of leftover firecrackers and small-arm explosives still sat for months in grocery fronts and delis as innocuously as a carton of eggs or a bag of flour. Evidently they looked too tempting to pass up.

Darren rumbled through the screen netting of the door and Jerry came out with his camera, filming the whole thing for some unknown posterity.

"What the fuck—" I said, taken aback by the brash echo of my own voice.

Nate and Luca erupted in laughter and collapsed into each other like crooked bookends. Nate rooted around in the front pocket of his Hawaiian shirt, then moved on to the pockets of his cargo shorts. He produced a slim yellow lighter and Luca immediately snatched it from his hands. He worked the silver coil a few times in his fingers before catching, and he touched the thin flame to the loose slack of rope that hung from the top of the firecracker like a candle's wick.

Firecracker lit, Luca quickly moved towards the guitar, jamming it inside the hollow base, and then ran back across the porch. We all had our fingers jammed into our ears like we were waiting for a bomb to go off. After a few seconds, the whole thing went up with a blast. Splintered wood chunks exploded and went flying in all directions. It felt excessive, the whole spectacle. The guitar's neck craned and hung limply over its body like a man with his head hung.

Nate was wailing again in the high-pitched laugh he reserved for especially drunk occasions. He and Luca exchanged triumphant high fives. Luca reached down into the plastic-wrapped 12-pack of Snow beer and placed two glass bottles into my hands.

"One for you, and one for your girlfriend," he sneered, laughing pleasantly to himself. He popped the top on both of them and waited with his arms crossed in front of me until I took a sip from each. Even among the foreigners, the pressure was sometimes hard to escape—certain occasions inevitably called for the introduction of alcohol.

As I turned to go back inside the house, Nate cut me off, standing between the door and me.

"So next year, it'll be just you and Grant and Jerry, huh," he said. I couldn't tell if he was the one wobbling or whether we both looked stable because I was off-balance too. I nodded.

"Too bad," he continued. "Those guys wouldn't know a party if it bit them in the ass. You'll be sad to lose all of us old guys."

"Yeah, of course," I said, still trying to work my way around him. "But we'll have a lot of new people coming."

"Two girls," Nate mused, looking lazily at the sky. "You gotta promise me something though." He outweighed me by fifty pounds and in that moment looked almost menacing in the doorway.

"You gotta promise me you won't start dating one of them, okay?"

The abruptness of his question caught me off-guard. "Promise you what?"

I asked.

"Rachel is my roommate and she's great," he said, composing himself again. "I don't want you dating one of the other foreigners after her." He had this genuine, almost tender, glare in his eyes that I almost didn't believe. I stared hard at him, wondering how long it would last.

"You know what I really want, though?" he asked. His eyes narrowed and he grabbed me at arm's length by the shirt collar. "I want you to fuck a bunch of Chinese girls. No more of this relationship shit."

My heart was pounding in my chest the way it did when I had a lot to drink. Knowing that I wouldn't be able to get past him otherwise, I took his hands in mine and drew him in close.

"For you Nate," I said, clapping him on the back, "anything."

We used to judge each week by the length of Nate's hair—long and unkempt meant a good drinking week and freshly washed meant we hadn't done our job well. In the moonlight, his hair looked like a lion's mane, coarse and blond, blowing in the wind.

"Don't you forget it," he said, stabilizing himself against the porch banister. He picked up an empty glass bottle and tomahawked it against a tree 20 meters away. Again he made the same high-pitched cackling noise, like an evil genius who had just spawned a monster.

It was a habit the guys had when they got drunk. I hated that they did it, but I couldn't say anything. Nate picked a few more bottles out of the small receptacle they kept outside of the house for recyclables. Some mornings, we'd hear the rattling of cans and clanging glass and know that some of the locals were making their rounds, collecting the bottles in order to recycle them at a small profit. We probably would have done it ourselves if we cared enough to find out where the nearest station was. Mostly, we figured they deserved it—they could certainly use the money more than we could.

"When you go inside, get Luca for me," Nate called out as I shouldered past him and got my hand on the doorknob. I slipped inside the bathroom and on the way out, I grabbed the suit jacket that I left slumped on the couch and headed back outside. I quickly walked the twenty paces past their stoop to my house. Already Luca and Darren had joined in with the bottle throwing and I could hear their voices carrying and mingling with the refrains of stray cats in the distance. The whole way, I heard the loud crash of the bottles as they shattered and collided with the ground. I thought about the elderly trash collectors the next day bending down to gather the broken shards—each one a piece of something bigger that was no longer whole.

At the door to my house, I checked for the keys in my pockets. After rooting around for close to a minute, I remembered that I had given them to Rachel and that she had probably locked them inside. My arms fell heavy at my sides and I let a deep sigh permeate the night air. Again I heard the sound of glass smashing against the stone tiles, and with the voices of the other male teachers getting louder, I turned and headed back toward Nate's house. Two bottles were still waiting for me on the porch sill. At the end of the day, it didn't matter what we did. There would always be someone to clean it up in the morning.

RESTLESS

The honeymoon ended—crashed and burned, really—halfway through day three. Prior to that, things were going quite well. Everything seemed at once mystifying and nostalgic, and I was still reeling from culture shock at having been swooped up from a rural town and been deposited in perhaps the biggest city in the world. Despite the fact that when I first arrived, I had practically forgotten how to speak Japanese, problems seemed nonexistent. If I wanted to go somewhere, there was nothing stopping me; if I wanted to buy anything, chances were close to certain that a nearby shop sold it. I was a veritable Charlie in the sprawling, ever-evolving chocolate factory that was Tokyo.

Being in a first-world country, where I could drink water out of the faucet, make physical contact with an actual toilet, and occasionally eat food off of the floor was a country as good as any to whet my appetite for all of the comforts of America. When I arrived, I was met with the kind of culture shock first-time visitors to New York feel finding themselves in the center of Times Square. Tokyo, a city I had visited briefly twice before, was remarkably more frenetic than the Japan I remembered from studying abroad in Osaka.

For four nights I stayed at a guesthouse located in the center of Shinjuku. The rooms were all on the third and fourth floors of an otherwise nondescript building. Each floor was home to twelve lodgers, and most rooms were predominantly male, save for one four-person room reserved for women. The first floor of the building hosted an innocuous-looking bar and restaurant, and walking up the back staircase to the secret elevator at the end of a long hallway felt like passing into a poor man's Batcave. It took me nearly an hour to find the place. Like most Japanese, the owners of the guesthouse put their trust in the integrity of residents; there was no reception desk or check-in service. The remote location of the rooms was the only measure preventing non-guests from sneaking in.

My room served the dual function of a dorm and a common area. Aside from the twelve beds arranged in six sets of bunks around the perimeter, it had a self-heating *kotatsu* underneath a square table where residents gathered to play cards; a mini-TV; and wireless internet. There were a couple of oversized bottles of *sake* there to serve the common good. In reality, it was hard to call what we stayed in "bunks." I slept on a *tatami* mat, a hard slab of approximately three inches, over which lay a thin *futon* comforter that separated me from the floor. For the purposes of my first four days in Japan, it was my proverbial bunker—my escape from nuclear fallout.

My bunkmate was an older Japanese man of 45 or 50. The first time I met him, he was lying on the top bunk, completely submerged in blankets. His head and hands were the sole exceptions peeking out over the top to connect noodle-spooled chopsticks to lips. Every once in a while he put down his disposable bowl of instant *ramen* to take sips from a can of Sapporo beer. In his ears were a pair of headphones attached to a cell phone in a tiny display holster. His eyes were fixed on the Japanese news program coming over the screen in short-wave flashes. In the utter quiet and solitude of the room, we didn't exchange a single word.

According to some of the other guests I talked to, my bunkmate had lived at the guesthouse for almost two years, an astounding amount of time given the general demographic that the place attracted—predominantly backpackers in their mid-20s on a budget who didn't mind staying in cramped quarters. Travelers who came to stay at the guesthouse usually did so for a maximum of a few days or weeks, earning my bunkmate the moniker of a "lifer."

It was clear that he had staked out the best corner of the room. Like a bear in hibernation, the man above me had packed an entire life's-worth of necessary vestiges into the 6' x 2' rectangle that he inhabited. Held on the rafters above his bunk were coat hangers bearing dress shirts and suit jackets. There was a space heater directed toward him from the opposing bedpost. Alarm clock, toiletries, spare batteries, miscellaneous supplies (rubber bands, pens), and nightclothes had been neatly prepared on a mock nightstand. Slid between two shelves of a plastic cupboard was a see-thru storage container full of clothing and other belongings. He even wrapped aluminum foil around the part of the fluorescent light directly facing him, to avoid having to look at it before lights out at 11:00 PM every night.

I found myself wondering how the man above me, especially at his age, could stand to live in a place like this for so long. There was no privacy, hardly a free space to move around, and an endless stream of tourists to put up with. But perhaps, then, it wasn't a choice. Maybe he had financial obligations—aging parents he had to put in a home, child support to pay to a divorced wife and kids, a large debt he had to repay from his younger days playing *pachinko*. I daresay that no one would choose to live like that if they could help it. What the man made up for in proximity to the city and metro fare, he paid for with having to perpetually live with eleven other strangers in a room that was not his own. In the end, I had to concede that in a city like Tokyo—where pedestrians don't jaywalk, shopkeepers never frown, and salary men routinely put in 60-hour workweeks—you could convince yourself of living through most anything.

I was sitting in a Doutor Coffee on the other side of Shinjuku when the realization struck me: *Tokyo is an extraordinarily lonely place to live*. Ironic, largely because it is one of the densest cities in the world population-wise, but aside from the sheer number of people, I had never felt more completely and unabashedly alone. Everyone seemed less concerned about the multitudes of other people living among them than they were about themselves and their own lives. For many people, especially young women, beauty and fashion superseded most other earthly needs, and included braving physical discomfort, cold, and hunger, simply to fit into a society that could be so callously judgmental.

I got the pervasive sense that I wasn't good enough. Everywhere I went, I was surrounded by people whose superficial façade to the world represented the sum total of their existence. Their clothes were slick, their hair was permed, and their painted faces were masks of cool distance—the impenetrable, impersonal gazes that isolate people from one another. It was this weighty, invisible silence that perpetually lingered in the air, broken only by the raucous carelessness of insobriety. I knew I needed a break from Tokyo, and that I needed to get away; I just didn't know how far away I would get.

Growing up, I'd had a romantic association with solo long-distance train travel. Throttling though space along a ceaseless span of metal track, there is a longing for a faraway place and the physical sensation of traveling hundreds of miles over a variety of terrains to get there. There is the ever-changing panorama of scenery, the hours left entirely to your own devices, and the gentle sway of the heated train lulling you in and out of sleep. Short-distance trips had become such a routine part of my life that I hardly flinched at the thought of a two or three-hour commute. But I had never embarked on a voyage where the journey filled me with as much exhilaration as the destination—a voyage where both the journey and the destination were new.

The destination itself was easy. Ever since I became interested in Japan, I had always wanted to go to Hokkaido, the northernmost island of Japan. Having done my research beforehand, I knew what I was getting myself into. The distance from Tokyo to Sapporo was a little over 500 miles and took just over 24 hours by local train. Once there, it would take at least another two hours to get to Kutchan, the small town where my friend Tim would be hosting me at the ski lodge where he worked. I liked the idea of having some introspection on the trip. I relished spending time with the other foreigners in Taigu, but constantly being around other people was making me crazy. *This will be perfect*, I reasoned. *Finally, some time alone to think.*

There would be no fewer than fourteen separate local train transfers, with a wait time ranging from a couple of minutes to over an hour at each stop along the train's route. The longest section would be the final leg—a seven-hour stretch on the *Hamanasu* express train via the Seikan Tunnel that connects the two islands of Honshu and Hokkaido. There were much faster ways of getting to Sapporo, not least of which included flying or taking the high-speed *shinkansen*, but those options were all two or three times more expensive. Besides, a large part of me wanted to feel the length of the journey, to tick off each hour knowing that the destination was just that little bit more within reach.

The trip began at 4:30 AM on the morning of my fourth and final night at the Shinjuku guesthouse. It was probably a mistake to stay up drinking *sake* with Nimrod and Svi, two Israelis I met who were on a two-month journey around the world, but already it felt like I had hardly spoken a word aloud in days. Most of the other people at the guesthouse smiled and nodded, but very few actually talked. Out on the street, there was even less of a chance of making conversation. Difficulties in communication in Japan far exceeded congenial social awkwardness and at times felt like a full-blown crisis.

We poured out tiny shot glasses from the almost comically large carafes of *sake*, and after a few *kampai*, we started airing our grievances about Japan—how immaculately clean everything was, how meticulously ordered. The fact that people wear N95 masks because they are terrified of getting sick. How every time you enter a store, shopkeepers berate you with honorific superlatives. That the sexual frustration has manifested itself into a society of off-color sexual practices that include everything from *hentai* to vending machines peddling used female undergarments. How Japan's suicide rate and rate of new patients infected with HIV are both the highest in any developed country. That there is enough bowing and politeness to feel that the Japanese are crippled by their own humility.

Instead of facing these problems and examining the mentality and emotional motives behind them, Japan applies a polished veneer over them. We talked about how they created women-only cars in the train, pushed social outcasts to the absolute fringes of society to avoid "tarnishing" their culture, failed to educate their children about safe sex practices and HIV prevention, and swept away everything illicit and seedy into a thriving underground subculture. There are people who consciously go against the mainstream, but they do so at a cost—often with a great deal of social stigma. Others do so by changing their physical appearance, with piercings or dyed hair or funky outfits, partly as a cry for attention. In the most extreme cases, people commit suicide.

The suitcase that I had packed was large and unwieldy and I regretted immediately the decision to bring it along. It followed me up and down stairs, into and out of train cars, and over and under turnstiles. I hardly remembered what was inside of it, only that there was no down jacket and no boots, two of the only things that would have been worth taking. If I found a seat on some of the longer routes, I kept it wedged between my knees, and put my head on top of it to sleep. The cars were warm and quiet and all I had to do was set an alarm for when we were slated to arrive at the next station.

In the slightly longer breaks, when I had 40 minutes or an hour before my next transfer, I got lunch or dinner at one of the station *kissaten,* or coffee shops. They often had a small selection of baked pastries—knotted croissants stuffed with red bean paste—or some tuna or cooked meat wrapped in a triangle of rice and dried seaweed. At some of the bigger stations, they had a dedicated stall serving various forms of noodles. In Sendai, six hours in, I bought a cheap bowl of *udon* with shrimp *tempura.* I punched in the order on a vending machine, fed it a few *yen* coins and brought the resulting ticket to the counter. As I was handing it to a woman wearing rubber gloves and a facemask, she pointed down, instructing me instead to put the ticket in a small basin on the table. She swooped it up and got to work making my order—no contact, not a single noise uttered.

A trip of this scale and to this exacting degree of accuracy would only have been possible in a country like Japan, where trains run so punctually that I hardly had to check where I was going so much as what times the various trains were leaving the stations. The sole exception was when we got stopped in Morioka near the northernmost tip of Honshu. Police had barricaded the automatic turnstiles, and there was a line of disgruntled and anxious ticket-holders stretching halfway down the station platform. Judging from the beleaguered expressions around me, it became increasingly more evident that any disturbance to the normally circadian train cycle was patently unbearable.

When the trains finally resumed, I discovered the cause of the hold-up—a suicide in front of the train had forced it to stop suddenly, release all of its passengers, and send in a crew to take care of the body. When the announcement flashed on the screens first in Japanese, and then in English, I was horrified. In Tokyo proper, suicides on the JR East Chuo Line are so common—almost daily—that there is even an announcement to alert passengers that they may experience a sharp brake and be asked to exit the train. Entry-level positions for the East Japan Railway are with working as part of the clean-up team. Most of the other people queued behind the turnstiles didn't show the least concern—it seemed they lamented the wait time more than the loss of a human life. The announcement called it a "human incident"—no one would admit what it really was.

The time passed much more slowly than I had envisioned. From the window of each train, I watched the landscape go through at least four distinct phases—from wheat-planted flatlands to small rural townships, and snow-covered evergreens to the cool serenity of the Pacific Ocean. The gradual rise in snow along the way was like a barometer of relative nearness to my final destination. At times I would wake up to an elevated level of snow on the ground and a small decrease in temperature. By the time I eventually got to Sapporo, it was a great deal chillier than where I'd started. Station signs in English had all but fallen away, showing only the ancient, typeset Japanese reserved for locals.

By the twelfth hour, I was reaching my breaking point. I began to feel pain shooting up and down my legs. I hated only being able to sleep for minutes at a time before being jolted awake by the next transfer point. I had a severe paranoia about missing my next train and getting stranded—of having to add yet more hours to the trip. Sometimes when I was bored or couldn't sleep anymore, I just pushed down on my legs, letting the flush tingly feeling return to my extremities. I tried to reason why I had wanted to do it in the first place: *Just think of the friendships you'll make, how much you'll learn about yourself, the greater appreciation you'll have for even the most mundane things in life…*

Every train I left, it felt like there were still so many more that I had yet to board—a revolving door of seats and faces. The scenery might be different but the experiences were always the same. At the door to each new train, I kept having this misguided hope that *this* would be the moment—that a kind stranger would approach me and the two of us would launch into a fascinating conversation. We would talk for so long that I would forget where I was going and wish I never had to leave Japan and return back to China. There would be a dramatic moment where I'd have to make a decision, and I'd use a version of the line I'd been practicing from *Before Sunrise*: *This is what we should do. You should get off the train with me here in Vienna, and come check out the capital.*

In twenty-seven hours, that moment never came. The trains were eerily silent, eating alone at meals was incredibly common, and it was rare for someone to go so far as to make any physical contact at all. No one cared that I was foreign or that I looked different or were even curious enough to whisper about me secretly to their neighbor. Perhaps part of me should have been grateful, relieved to have finally succeeded in sliding under the radar, but it did just the opposite: it left me feeling empty. Maybe all I needed was some validation, some acknowledgment of my worth. On the whole trip, I never saw another foreigner. There was no motion picture-worthy banter, nor even any casual acquaintances to be made. For the entire twenty-seven hours, I didn't utter a single word.

I never did consider scrapping my ticket back to China, but I did on more than one occasion think about a life in Japan. There was a lot about China that I didn't like—the pushing and shoving on the trains, the fact that customers yell to get the wait staff's attention at a restaurant, the pervasive dirt and grime—but somehow even those dislikes started to become less agitating than they were endearing. They were all *real* things. Nothing was sterilized or dumbed down—people, interactions, filth, poverty, environmental hazards—were all up close and in your face. Despite all the beautifying of Beijing for the Olympics, China couldn't help but bear its true self.

But if China was everything that Japan was not, then perhaps Japan was everything that China wished it were—a country with a very large middle class, no problematic alliances with Western powers, and a society in which almost no one questions the government. Inherent in all of my griping and naysaying was a paradox:

Why would I resent a country that stands for everything that is commonly thought to be good? Clean facilities, impeccable service, useful innovations—rarely does a day pass when one encounters real difficulty or the sense that one thing or another is not exactly in its rightful place. In fact, nearly every precaution is taken to ensure a smooth, carefree existence. What defense did I have except, perhaps, that too much comfort could be a bad thing?

I saw hundreds of people on the train. For the most part, no one willingly sat next to me unless there were no other seats available, and even then, some still chose to stand. But from my vantage, I got a good survey of the various passengers—retired folks, ski and snowboard enthusiasts, couples on vacation, commuting businessmen. The majority were students on their way to or from school. It was easy to spot them in their uniforms—the boys all in letter jackets and slacks, the girls in thigh-high skirts and high-heeled boots that laced up the front. It didn't matter that it was below freezing out—it was as if they had turned a blind—fastidiously outlined—eye to the cold. For hours it was all I could see—checker-print skirts and the garish innocence they tried to hide.

There was one girl that I remembered in particular. It was sixteen hours in, on my way to Aomori, when I saw her. She looked to be about my age. She was tall, indifferent, and strikingly overweight, wrapped in a thick parka that swallowed her belly and brushed up against her thighs. It was clear that she could care less what anyone thought of her. She wore long pink polka-dotted snow pants that went down to her ankles. Her hair was a deep blue and piercings lined the entire length of her left ear. Her face was buried in her coat and her legs were crossed one thick boot in front of the other. She was sitting alone at the end of a long bench of an empty train car.

I didn't know her, and yet, I felt like we shared this kinship—like two outcasts in a foreign land. I had no idea if she felt the way I did, but I wanted to believe it, to think that there was someone else in the world that could understand me. It's weird, but the first thing I thought about was the suicide in the front of that train—that perhaps this girl was feeling just as misunderstood, just as lonely. I wanted so desperately to go up to her, to put my hands on her fat face and tell her that she was real and that she was a person and that even if no one else did, I cared about her for the simple reason that she existed.

But of course, I didn't say any of that. After a few stops, she stood up and got off the train. Her snow pants made a loud, swishing noise as she scurried to get through the doors, and I looked around to see if anyone else had noticed but no one was paying attention. For long stretches after that, I stopped looking at people. Instead, I listened to *Bridge Over Troubled Water* on a pair of beaten headphones. I kept pausing it after the song "The Only Living Boy in New York." I loved that one line: *Half of the time we're gone but we don't know where.* Peering out over the expanse of Japanese countryside, I mused over whether or not it was real—that feeling of leaving but not really having gone. I wondered what it might feel like to set out in the world and be the only person there. Then, pretty soon, I didn't have to imagine anymore.

CLARITY

Some Shansi Fellows seem to have a sense of failure just before the end of the first year of teaching and work. A year has gone by and there is so much left to do. You haven't been studying as well as you should have been so your language seems primitive; your teaching is not as good as it should be; you haven't made as many friends as you should have; or there were offers of friendship you just didn't take up.

Possibly for the first time in your life you have begun to evaluate yourself. No one else seems to be evaluating you. You might feel an urgency to know whether Shansi is evaluating you. You will want to know what the standards are. The standards are those you set for yourself, and they are the standards of the "real world."

You will probably find your soul somewhat restored by a summer vacation trip and a great sense of accomplishment will begin to build as you check off the miles traveled and sights seen.

In late summer or early fall, the new Fellows begin to arrive. All of a sudden you are the authority on everything for the fledgling arrival. You know the ropes. You know everything compared to what the new Fellows know. They think you know everything. You will have to accept a great deal of responsibility for their first contacts with the country. You will again see things from their new perspective and realize just how far you have come in such a short time. It will be a very fulfilling experience and the tendency might be to go overboard and help at every juncture. But you will realize that you have to give some room for personal growth as well. Knowing where the dividing line is can be difficult.

HOMECOMING

I had never seen Taigu half as beautiful: hot, but not nearly as humid and muggy as my summer of travel had been—still warm enough for shorts in the daytime, but clear with a crisp chill in the air at night. I was going through intense travel withdrawal—missing the thrill of seeing new places and experiencing new things. But in spite of the shoving and shouting, the poverty and the dust, the censorship and the corruption, it felt cathartic to be home. While travelling, it had always felt like something wasn't right—a tingling sort of anxiety, like sandpaper under my skin. It was coming home in a literal sense. But it was also a visceral homecoming—I felt connected to Taigu, now that my first year, replete with struggle, challenge, and triumph, was safely under my belt.

Starting my second year, I felt like I was looking at Taigu through a fresh set of eyes. All the familiar sights and people seemed newly animated. Old students were re-imagined—some as more distant acquaintances following the long break, and others as full-blown friends without the "student" signifier. Restaurants may well have been serving up dishes that we were trying for the first time. Of course, newest of all was the shake-up in the ranks of foreigners who lived together on campus.

Nate, Rachel, Darren, and Luca were gone, but in their place came a wave of fresh foreign teachers. There were two girls that year: Tyra and Raina. Tyra graduated the same year as I did from Oberlin, but she took a year off to live with her boyfriend in Chicago. She had worked as a barista at a fancy coffeehouse there, but in her off-hours secretly yearned to be an artist. Raina was a fresh graduate like myself when I first arrived—and her youth showed. She didn't speak any Chinese prior to arriving, and already I could tell that it would be a challenging year for her. The German teacher position wasn't renewed that year—something about the school not having enough funds for the program—but there was one other American—Dylan—tall, lanky, and fiercely smart—who took Darren's place and took up residence in his old room.

In the midst of all these changes, Grant and I found ourselves in a new position of leadership—no longer wayward sheep herded around by our own Senior Fellows, but shepherds ourselves, with a small flock at our beck-and-call. It was strangely empowering to be the authority on a place. Whereas one-year prior, I knew close to nothing about Taigu and had to rely almost entirely on Nate and Rachel to get around, I was amazed by how much I could now transmit to others.

More than that, there was this sense of familiarity—that, in some ways, I knew what I could expect from my second year. Somewhere along the way, things just started to make sense. I was in charge of the decisions and what activities we did as a group and I also understood the way Taigu worked: how to cope with the little surprises and disappointments that occupied each day, how everything seemed to go wrong at the last minute, letting go of any claim to even the slightest shred of privacy or personal space, and how to interact with the people who populated this tiny town at the edge of the world.

Still, there were occasions when all the experience in the world wasn't enough—where my perceived "expertise" was put to the test and failed. Situations ranged from the ordinary to the ridiculous; worst was when I got us stranded in the capital city of Taiyuan for the night without any way back home. My Junior Fellows were there, looking up at me with the same wide-eyed reverence with which I had reserved for my own Senior Fellows. But aside from filling me with a bloated sense of assurance, being the "authority" made me acutely aware of all the things I could not do.

It was an interesting role reversal. When I had talked with Rachel the previous year about my lack of excitement for my second year and the new Fellows, she told me that one year prior she had felt the same way—that coming back to Taigu from a long summer holiday filled her with equal parts dread and anxiety, fear of what was to come, and disappointment at potentially not meeting her first year's expectations. I was also nervous about returning to Taigu—but for different reasons. Taigu was the closest place I'd had to home in over four years, but I was anxious about how different that home would feel. It was the people who made the place, and Nate, Rachel and Darren—three friends who had been as close as siblings—were gone. I had no idea how I would reconcile the weight of their absence.

Rachel's leaving, though, was the hardest to negotiate. It didn't help that nearly everywhere on campus had some connection with her—and that I could spool memories from even the most mundane occurrences. It was not only that I missed her, the comfort of not feeling alone, but that I didn't really know what Taigu was like without her. Trips to the underground supermarket, buying a milk tea after dinner, staying up late lesson planning for the next day's class—none of it felt right.

It was an enormous comfort, though, to still have Grant and Jerry there. I was shocked at how close Grant and I grew, like our time apart had actually made us miss living with each other. In some ways, he acted as a surrogate for the void caused by Rachel. In addition to going to the gym, we left almost every morning to go to class together and waited until the other was finished teaching to walk back home. We had gone so far that the others started referring to us like we were this quintessential married couple, squabbling over how much to spend on new furniture for the house and divvying up chores for every time we had guests over.

For that whole first week back, Grant had been baking muffins. Each day, I helped him take an armload full of raw materials—eggs, flour, bananas, baking powder, and water—to the main teaching building and set them up in his classroom. As I went across the hall to start my own class, he led a couple of students back home for a second trip to bring over a collapsible round table and a small toaster oven containing a flat baking tin and a muffin tray. For the lesson, Grant went over the requisite cooking vocabulary on the board and proceeded to demonstrate the cooking words involved with making muffins in class—cutting, pouring, mixing, stirring, baking. At the end of class, he let them try the fruits of their labor—warm, fragrant, and altogether foreign.

My lesson that week was considerably less interesting. I was trying a fresh topic with my new students on travel and was soliciting "most interesting" stories from my students' summer vacations. In the process, I told them about my own adventures, presenting a collection of 50 photos and a stack of foreign bills and coins from the various countries I had visited. Inherent in my lesson, though, was a fair degree of guilt, both with respect to my disposable income as a teacher and the relative ease of mobility afforded by my passport. Though some of my students expressed no interest in travel at all, I couldn't help but feel bad for those that did—the sons and daughters of rural farmers who would probably never have the opportunity to leave the country in their lifetimes.

The answers I received really should not have surprised me. For more than 90 percent of my students, their responses fell into a handful of general categories: they spent time with their family, attended their high school reunion, watched TV, attended a friend's wedding, played computer games, got drunk and did karaoke, helped with chores around the house, cooked meals for their parents (some, for the first time ever), or looked after aging grandparents or new nieces and nephews. One of my English majors excitedly related a story about playing mahjong with some of her friends.

"At the end of the game," she said, "the loser had a punishment." She paused and scanned the room, suppressing a laugh with her hands. "They had to drink cold water!"

The room erupted in laughter, as if unable to fathom a more embarrassing lot.

To be fair, theirs weren't too far from the activities that typified my own life in Taigu, but the mundane quality of their activities didn't do much to inspire confidence in my students' creativity. Very few of them left their hometown at all during the break. It doesn't help that China does a uniquely bad job of fostering travel. Students and working people all have vacations at the same time during the same national holidays, so even China's usually very efficient train and bus system is no match for the gridlock.

With little in the way of sightseeing in Taigu, the closest thing I got was on local buses through town. As opposed to the big cities I saw on my travels, or even in the provincial capital, Taiyuan, there were no markers of famous sites or tourist attractions. Instead, there were bus stop names indicating local landmarks like "Agricultural Bank of China" or "Shanxi Agricultural University, Student Dormitories." On one bus trip on my way to *Jia Jia Li*, I saw a traditional farmer funeral going on in the street. It was maybe the second time I had ever seen one—a procession led by old men and women (presumably good friends of the deceased) dressed in white head scarves and robes covering the majority of their bodies. Their heads were bowed and their hands adopted a praying position in front of their chests. Behind them, a caravan of white pick-up trucks adorned with large peacock-colored wreaths bore through town, obscuring the flow of traffic.

My assignment on travel, as well as Grant's baking lesson, made up a couple of lessons I came to coin as "greatest hits." At the beginning of the year, there were mock restaurant lessons centered on ordering food. Around Halloween, there was pumpkin carving in class. For a clothing lesson, we came in wearing four or five layers of tops, bottoms, and accessories and proceeded to strip each one of them off to the simultaneous delight and horror of our students. A topic on marriage and dating yielded both a speed dating exercise as well as a marriage-counseling skit in which pairs of couples gave the fictitious reasons for why they wanted a divorce. Every class was a bit like performing comedy—with each repetition a chance to fine tune the material. These were the kinds of lessons that had been passed down for years among each generation of foreign teachers. Like a gigantic game of telephone, the best lessons were those that had survived through oral history with minor changes made along the way. A similar thing could have been said about our day-to-day lives.

Each of us in Taigu essentially had the same life: we all taught the same number of hours at about the same times, lived in the same kinds of houses, and took the same vacation dates. We had meals together, shared the same friends, and participated in the same group activities. Even for Fellows in years past, I had to guess that only minor tweaks had been made to the same general formula. An old favorite restaurant went out of business and was replaced with a new one. Some exciting new fad enchanted the group for a week before falling out of favor. New Chinese friends were made to account for those who had come before and graduated. Every winter, snow fell, and every fall, dust storms blew in from the north. There wasn't that much flexibility to work outside of the box. New Fellows came and went, but Taigu, and, indeed, Shanxi Agricultural University, more or less remained unchanged.

Though I hadn't stopped trying to challenge myself, I couldn't help but feel that since being back, the things I was doing in Taigu weren't especially new or groundbreaking. As a town, Taigu had hardly budged in the two months I was away. One of my former students said it best when he quipped, "the restaurants are still bright and gaudy and the road still looks like shit." It made for a depressing first week back, but for exactly that reason, there was a certain comfort that came with being in a familiar place. I never realized how much I genuinely *liked* China until I came back this time around.

When we all arrived from vacation, Tyra, one of the new teachers, surprised me when she lamented that she had "stolen Rachel's life." It was true that she had inherited Rachel's room, her job, her friends, one of her cats, and even some of her old belongings. Greeting her by the front door were Rachel's old pair of slippers. I hadn't really ever thought of it that way before, but the same was true of all of us. I had stolen Brian's life and in a year's time, someone would be arriving to steal mine and everything that came with it.

For dinner one night we all went to the Pingyao restaurant in town, Nate's old favorite, and had a big meal there with a bunch of Chinese friends. As might be expected, Grant, Jerry, and I couldn't help talking about our first year—the stories and memories that comprised our shared friendship. And in some ways, it was still like old times—we all drank too much and took embarrassing videos of each other. But then there were the differences: this time there were no indulgent speeches, no discussions on obscure video games, and no over-the-top singing of "Just a Friend" by meal's end.

Probably the most challenging and frustrating part of the Fellowship was the fact that no one was there to tell us if we were doing a good job or not or what made a meaningful experience and what didn't. Like our lesson plans, the best tidbits about what past Fellows had done got filtered down, but it was our job to interpret and make sense of those stories. Ultimately, it was up to each of us to decide our Fellowship for ourselves, and that was something that couldn't be passed down or replicated.

More and more, I kept feeling like I had one foot in one world and one in another. Already, I was beginning to fantasize about life back in America. Grant and I went ahead and started a new yearlong lifting regimen, knowing full well that we wouldn't be there long enough to see it through to completion. Such was the feeling that consumed my everyday: *Why start something that you know you can't finish? Why foster new friendships that will only be doomed to failure? Why keep studying Chinese when you will only fall behind in America?*

One night, I just started walking with no particular destination in mind. I passed the student dorms, dark and ominous, like the giant concrete hulls of wrecked ships—and kept walking, leaving the gates of the university behind me. I realized that I no longer felt trepidation at the darkness of Taigu's rural countryside. I let my feet guide me and trusted my instincts to navigate those uncertain paths back to safety. That's when it hit me: unlike the transience of travel, this—Taigu—was my life, and that no matter what the future had in store for me, I had to live out the next year with the resolve of one facing an ever expanding *present*, laid out before me like patched cobblestone streets, brick smokestacks, and fiery pink sunsets.

DON'T DRINK
THE WATER

"You know, you *really* remind me of someone." The man in the blue and white Billabong swim trunks stared hard at me and pointed, nodding slowly and wagging his finger up and down rhythmically with his head. He was squatting above a small fire, his ass dangerously close to the flames. Droplets of water were falling from his skin and gathering in the pit below. He had one eye open and the other half-closed, searching hard to draw a connection.

"I got it!" he shouted, hopping up and down over the fire. "Keanu Reeves. You look *just* like Keanu Reeves." The man spoke in a thick British accent, and at first I thought he had said that I looked like "canoe reeds," which I found to be both perplexing and somewhat offensive. I looked over at Tyra and shook my head, laughing. She was chuckling too, taking straw sips from a squat bucket of mixed alcohol and fruit juice that the bartender had handed her. She leaned over and put her hand on my knee, as if to take pity.

"You know that movie he was in with the bus, and they were driving really fast and then Keanu Reeves was all like, 'You're crazy! You're fuckin' crazy!'" He was doing the voice and waving his arms from side-to-side and looked like he was going to lose his balance and topple backwards into the fire at any moment. The friend he had come with was sitting on a log facing Tyra and me, and was trying hard not to laugh. He pulled a Ziploc baggie of tobacco and another smaller one of marijuana from a waterproof dry sack and started to roll a spliff on his lap.

"*Speed?*" I asked quizzically, never having seen the movie.

"Yes, that's it!" Again, the man was jubilant. "You look just like Keanu Reeves in *Speed.*" I sat back on the log, silently mulling over the comparison in my head.

"Just because he's half-Asian doesn't mean he looks like Keanu Reeves," Tyra crooned, herself more than a bit tipsy. She placed the lime green bucket on my lap and extended her arms out towards the fire.

"That's not what I'm saying," the man replied defensively. "I didn't even know the bloke was Chinese or whatever he is." Having warmed up temporarily, he waddled out from around the flame, making a point of sticking his ass out and shaking it, eliciting jeers from the three of us, as well as the Laotian guys standing behind the bar.

The bar was the last one along the tubing circuit down the Nam Song River. Vang Vieng was infamous for its primary tourist draw—slow-paced rafting on giant inflatable inner tubes. With the increasing popularity came the requisite facilities—countless bars lined either side of the river and enterprising shopkeepers threw lines—long slacks of rope attached to a water bottle—to lure partygoers to pay a visit. Most also had slides or rope swings set-up nearby. Others had tables for beer pong. It was almost impossible to imagine what the town of 25,000 was like before foreigners converged on it. The tourists were the clientele, and they made all the rules.

The man sat back down on the log next to his friend. I smiled weakly and shrugged my shoulders at Tyra, and she took the pail from my lap by the handle.

"So, how long have you two been together?" the man asked, hugging his arms tightly around his exposed midsection. His hair, knotted in thick dreadlocks, hung loosely over his shoulders and his stomach was thin and stretched tight like the skin of a canvas drum. He wore a long beaded necklace that dangled down to his navel.

"A month," I told him, even though the real answer was more complicated. Tyra and I started seeing each other at the beginning of my second year in Taigu, but we hadn't been exclusive until deciding to travel together over winter break. For a long time, she still had a boyfriend in the states with whom she talked regularly over Skype. It didn't bother me much considering that he was thousands of miles away and that my situation was hardly any better—I had just gotten out of a serious relationship with Rachel. Once, a while after Tyra and I had already seen each other naked, she undressed in front of the webcam for her boyfriend. The feeling was so unsettling, she told me, that she knew she had to end it.

The whole thing with Tyra caught me by surprise. Rachel and I broke up after our last night in Taigu, both knowing that long distance wouldn't work. It took me a long time to get over her, and together, Tyra and I talked a lot about our situations—how we were both dealing with this void that couldn't easily be filled. The whole time, it was like our roles had been flipped—Tyra was the over-eager Junior Fellow and now I was the Senior Fellow who had already done a Taigu romance. I wasn't sure how Tyra felt except that we both had these unresolved feelings and no one with whom to share them.

The man looked transfixed as he stared at the flames, like it was a living, breathing creature. He started talking to neither one of us in particular.

"I ask because—and don't take this the wrong way or anything—but how are you two actually together?" Tyra and I both stared back at him confused.

"I mean, you guys don't match at all. You don't even look like a couple. Look at your skin color." I looked down—an uncharacteristic chestnut auburn spread across my chest and arms. We had been in Laos for a week and evidently the sun was doing its job. I glanced over at Tyra. She always lamented the fact that she could never tan. Her skin retained the same white ivory glow regardless of the season, and she burned easily. She sat tugging at her loose skin as if it had been stained.

"Just look at the two of them," he cackled, his voice high-pitched and embellished. He signaled for his friend, but the other man was deep in concentration. A rush of adrenaline pumped through my chest and I felt my heartbeat quicken. I hadn't been in a fight since I was seventeen, but this was different. I knew that I didn't want to provoke the guy. He looked to out-age me by at least eight years and though I may have been bigger than him, the man was drunk and unstable and I didn't know what he was capable of. I let a long breath pass through my lips. There was always a tumultuous, intimidating quality to travel, and Laos was the first country Tyra and I visited together outside of China.

"Tom, what are you saying now?" The man's friend began, as if he had just become aware of the conversation. He had finally finished getting the spliff rolled and held up a lighter that he pulled out of the same waterproof sack.

"You're drunk, aren't you, Tom?" He droned out the word drunk, like it was an incantation.

"I'm not dru—" Tom began.

"I'm sorry about my friend Tom here," his friend told us, putting the spliff to his lips. "Don't pay any mind to what he's saying. He's just a little drunk, that's all."

Tom's own arms were the kind of leathery brown it takes days baking in the sun to attain. He lifted them up in the air, almost dazzled at the sight. I contemplated leaving then and there, packing up the tubes and going back down the Nam Song. But I didn't want to give him the satisfaction. We had gone through a lot of trouble to get there and he wasn't about to ruin the experience for us. I took Tyra's hand and whispered low enough for the other two not to hear: *It doesn't mean anything. He's not worth it.* Still, some part of me wanted to give him the benefit of the doubt. *Maybe there were no interracial couples in the U.K. Maybe he didn't know any better.*

The place was called Bob Marley Bar, and, true to its name, boasted a playlist replete with "Buffalo Soldier" and "No Woman, No Cry." Further upstream, bar decks were lined with girls mingling in two-piece bikinis and guys doing flips off of double-decker towers into the water. Most looked to be college students on vacation or older twenty-somethings desperate to retain their youth. Before we got to the bar, Tyra and I passed a bunch of them crossing a suspension bridge that led down to the water. One guy, covered head-to-toe in body paint with the words "Tubing Makes Girls Wet" in red marker across his chest cheered triumphantly and put his hand up as if to slap mine. When I raised my arm, he cast his aside, a deep roar resonating from his jowls. I looked down at the river. The banks had overflowed and the water had taken on a deep brown, the color of dysentery.

It was as if everyone I had ever despised from middle school rounded up their fraternity brothers and made a pilgrimage out to Southeast Asia. What united them more than age or association, though, was attitude. Everyone seemed to have this blithe indifference to everything, to want to "out-mellow" the next. Laos, a country where almost nothing was done with a sense of urgency, was the perfect cure for the frenzied pace of the everyday. No one seemed to mind that tourism had, if not destroyed the town's culture, at least drastically reinvented it. Drugs were getting into the hands of kids. The environmental effects of the partying culture were taking a toll on the Nam Song. Loud music was marring the town's level placidity. Safety, too, was a concern—I read that twenty-two tourists had drowned in the river the previous year.

Tom and his friend passed the spliff between them and exhaled deeply at the sky. In long drawn-out sentences, he told us the story of how this was the eighth day he had spent tubing, and how two days prior, he was taken in for questioning by the Vang Vieng police for possession of marijuana. They took his passport and said that they would hold onto it indefinitely unless he paid the equivalent of $600. His other option was a year-and-a-half behind bars. I looked back and forth at the two of them smoking, wholly unconcerned.

"So I'm basically stuck here." Tom took another long drag. "Might as well make the best of it." He rifled through his dry bag, at last uncovering a thick pouch stuffed with Euro notes.

"I'm also broke," he said, a smile forming across his face. "Used all my kip in the last week while the police had my passport."

I wanted to ask Tom how he could possibly be so blasé about losing his only form of international identification, or about having a criminal record in a country where he didn't know any of the laws, but I kept my mouth closed.

"This is my mate's money. He let me hold onto it for safekeeping. Doesn't hurt to have a bit of insurance, don't it?" He pulled out the first bill—a stiff red ten Euro note and waved it in the air, looking like he might soon burn through the whole stack.

"How many mushroom shakes for this?" Tom shouted over the music. The guys gathered behind the bar perked up and took notice.

"What do you want?"

"Mushroom shakes. How many for this?" He held the foreign note higher, like it had the weight of the wind and the sky behind it.

The bartender held up two fingers.

"Perfect," Tom said, and the bartender scooted out among the gravelly rocks and plucked the bill from his hands.

On a wall behind the bar was a list of prices for drinks. Most of the beer ran between eight and ten thousand *kip* (about a dollar). Buckets were 15,000 (unless you wanted top-shelf alcohol which was another 5,000). Shots of lao-lao, the Laotian rice whisky, were six. It was only if you got up close, that, tucked on the bottom half of the menu, and obscured by the rectangular counter, was the "secret" menu. "Happy shakes"—alcohol mixed with hash—ran 30,000 and mushroom shakes were 40,000. Still, this was considerably less than the ten Euros the bartender extorted from the Brit, but both parties seemed happy with the transaction.

I felt guilty that I couldn't just let loose like everyone else. Maybe this type of hedonistic excess wasn't for me, I thought. I realized that Tyra and I were a pair of unlikely tourists when it came to Vang Vieng. The makings of a good time were all there—drinking, dancing, music—and yet, something didn't feel right. I had misgivings about the ethics of it all. I was astounded by the inequality of everything— the way foreigners seemed to hold all the power. Vang Vieng had a system where all of the households were divided into ten village units, each taking its turn on a ten-day rotation to rent inner-tubes to tourists. But even then there was a cost—to the town, other industries, the communities in which they lived. They had developed a mutually dependent relationship with the tourists, and I wondered whether it would actually be better or worse if we were all sent packing tomorrow.

Still, we had known exactly what we would be getting into when we went there. On the river earlier that day, we saw the dense clumps of inner tubes rocking lazily downstream. Most of the floaters lay passively, taking sips from their own plastic pails. It was the dry season, so trips down the river were expected to take about three hours, compared with one during the rainy season. Bar owners threw lines at us from every direction—the competition for business was fierce. Outside, the air was still warm, but the water was cold. Paddling was useless given the slow tide, and the tubes were engineered so that it was impossible not to make contact with the river at all times. On a big sign approaching the bar from around a bend in the river were the words "Last Call." It was our last chance to fit in. We grabbed hold of the line and got pulled ashore.

After Tom placed his order, I stood up and ordered a beer from the bar, trying to get in the spirit. The bartender snapped off the cap and poured the beer into a tall plastic cup that he fished from behind the counter. Next, I saw him take a plastic cup full of ice and shove it into the blender. From under the counter, he pulled out a plastic tray heaping with mushrooms—all about the length and width of my index finger. He judiciously plucked the ones he thought fitting from the pile and added them to the blender. The mushroom caps looked snug and warm atop the scraggly stalks, like a winter hat. He poured a long stream of sugar from a bag on the counter and hit "pulse." After a few seconds, he poured out the frothy, gray mixture into two more plastic cups and walked them over to Tom.

"Thanks, mate," Tom said to the bartender. "Cheers." Tom handed the other drink to his friend. He looked back at Tyra and me.

"Have you guys every tried a mushroom shake?" The two of us shook our heads. "Well, come now, you should have some. You can't say you've been to Laos and never tried one. This is the real deal." We both shook our heads again.

"Really?" Tom asked us again, pleadingly. "You're going to regret it later."

"No thanks," I said, a little aggressively. "We're really not interested." The two men turned to each other and put down half of the shake in one gulp. Meanwhile, Tyra and I were just about finished with the bucket. I had drunk about half of it, but the slushy mixture looked and tasted like synthetic motor oil. When it sloshed from side-to-side, it had the same metallic glow. Tyra and I huddled closer to the fire.

Earlier that day a garbage truck had been moored, rendered immovable in the middle of the river. The water was shallow enough that the truck sank down to the bottom, and it wasn't going anywhere. I had no idea how it got there, but I hazarded to guess that it had something to do with the tourists. A group of guys, all wearing fake Ray-Bans and "Tubing in the O" tank tops, tried to muscle it out of the water, some jumping on the bed of the truck full of black garbage bags to add weight, while others pushed from the bottom. It seemed painfully obvious, but because they were in the water, they couldn't get an ounce of traction. I didn't stay long enough to see if the truck ever budged.

Back in town the night prior, we saw girls wearing Brazilian bikinis and ordering banana pancakes with peanut butter from food carts off the street. The first time I saw it, I thought it was this local dessert, and I marveled at how much our two cultures shared. It was only later that I realized how much of ourselves we instinctively project abroad, that our reach is almost limitless in its quest for the familiar. The truth was that none of us came to Vang Vieng to be adventurous. We were there to be overindulgent tourists who didn't give a damn about anything. We were all just playing our parts. In that way, Tom from Britain had succeeded where Tyra and I failed.

"Don't drink the water," Tyra said after a time.

"What," I asked.

"Don't drink the water." She wore this surly look that I had never seen before, and her eyes looked faraway and distant. "If you do, pretty soon you won't be thirsty." I heard what she was saying but the words didn't make any sense.

"What does the water have to do with it?"

"Nothing," she said. She started toying with the silver clasp on her bathing suit. Then, she added: "I feel sort of funny."

The pieces started to click into place. I felt myself get woozy and start to lose balance. I looked at the green bucket sitting empty on the ground. *No one ever washes these things out.* Then I remember saying out loud: "I don't think it was the water."

It was getting late and I knew we had to get out of there. I was frantic—getting ready to grab Tyra and round up the inner tubes—when all at once, it occurred to me that I desperately had to use the bathroom. As calmly as I could muster, I sauntered up to the bar. But when I looked behind the counter, the bartender was gone and in his place were a group of three teenage boys dressed in identical black shirts. They were smoking joints and eating mushroom caps straight off the stems. How long had they been there? "Lively Up Yourself" came on over the stereo speakers.

"Where is the bathroom?" I asked, a look of panic coming over my face.

One of the boys—no older than twelve—pulled a long stalk from his mouth and pointed at a small hut overlooking the ridge. He gave me a wink and focused his energy back on the tray of mushrooms in front of him.

My sandals were gone, and I was scrambling barefoot up the crooked path to get there. The rocks felt hard and jagged and were piercing my skin. When I finally reached the top and started peeing on a white porcelain slab inside the thatched hut, I noticed that my piss was bright orange, the color of polyurethane. Did I imagine it? I felt like I was being transported somewhere. The wailing cries of music and the shouts of distant partygoers were suddenly inaudible. I looked up in front of me and instead of the thick cluster of bars and inner tubes, there was a vast wheat field that seemed to stretch for miles across the plains. The sun would be setting soon, and already the bright orange ball of light was descending over the horizon.

The field stretched far back into the mountains and ran up against these soaring karst peaks that seemed to rise straight up from the water. The wheat was at least four feet high, and bushy stalks of goldenrod buckled and swayed in the light wind. I squinted into the sun and I thought I could make out a farmer, holding a rake and donning a straw hat. He was tending to his crop as if it were the most natural thing. Perhaps that was the way it used to be—this whole place. The locals had put their faith in tourists not to mess things up, and this was what happened. Did they predict it all along? What did it mean for the two of us to be there?

I re-fastened my belt, left the hut, and made quick, calculated steps down the path back to the river. Suddenly the image of the guesthouse we had been staying at in town flashed into my mind. On the front door was a sign that read, "Rent this room for a week, a month, or the rest of your life!" I had visions of the people who never left, the glassy-eyed hippies who lounged at Western cafés eating French toast and omelets—and the countless locals who needed them to stay exactly that way.

I WON'T BE HOME FOR CHRISTMAS, AGAIN

It occurred to me that receiving coal for Christmas in Taigu might not be the worst thing in the world. Coal powered everything, and I figured that a stocking-full could at least heat a moderately sized home for the majority of a day. By the looks of things, we all got coal in our stockings that year—coal dust in the air, coal energy in our pipes, coal stacked high in mounds where we lived, and even coal on the trains from workers who shoveled the black stuff into furnaces at stop points.

Growing up with my family in Brooklyn, we didn't have many traditions—no tree past age ten (it became too much of a hassle in our small apartment), no church services, and no holiday ham. We didn't even put out milk and cookies for Santa. When I was younger, I used to window-shop down Fifth Avenue with my mom, taking careful note of the elaborate displays in storefront windows. In more recent years, the only real Christmas tradition I had was walking with my friend Sam to the gigantic tree on 48th Street from his apartment in Greenwich Village, all while swigging warm brandy eggnog from a thermos to keep from freezing on the four-mile trek.

Christmases in years past saw me, most notably, playing guest at my cousin's birthday party—which fell on the twenty-fifth—as we helped to unpack and re-construct their plastic Christmas tree and decorate it with tiers of gaudy gold and silver tinsel, frosted glass bulbs, and Disney-themed ornaments. My uncle's house practically shouted holiday festivity—as the sound of Kenny G and Nat King Cole steadily pumped in from the TV speakers. The grown-ups spent the better part of the day in the kitchen—my uncle cooking, my mother quietly peeling vegetables, and my aunt making off-handed comments about my mom's dishwashing technique and how she needed to get a real job.

Each time, I looked forward to the chance to spend time with my cousin Emma, whom I only got to see once or twice a year. Emma's family only lived a couple of hours from us in Queens, but somehow it was always this logistical nightmare for our families to make time for each other. The yearly gathering was perhaps the closest thing to a reunion my family got, where the cousins and aunts I hadn't seen since the previous year's party all came out to celebrate Christmas and their prodigal niece. I was never sure what made me more uneasy, the fact that I was expected to make conversation with adults I hardly knew or that those adults were giving me presents I felt I hardly deserved.

At these sorts of occasions there was always a musical interlude, where two of my second cousins, my cousin Emma, my sister, and I would each take turns playing our various instruments to the amusement of the crowd. It was a relatively unbiased way of assessing our audible worth, which would then be extended to our other qualities. I played the cello, my sister the violin, and my three cousins (all about my age) played the piano. Because of the size of my instrument, I always performed last, but, by then, there was hardly anyone left in the audience who had any interest in whatever slapdash rendition of Handel or Mozart I could put together without sheet music.

At the end of the night when nearly all the guests had left to go home, my sister and I would beg my mother to stay overnight, no matter how much we knew she hated sleeping there, away from her own bed. Some years she would relent, but on others, she held fast, and we would trudge through the snow to the nearest subway stop and ride the two hours back home. Each year, we had the same feeling when we came back to our tree-less, decoration-less apartment—a feeling of not being good enough.

As it turned out, my mom and my sister didn't make it to my cousin's house for Christmas my second year in Taigu. It was only the second time in over a decade that they had missed the party. The day after Christmas was marked by a blizzard, blanketing the city with snow, and in typical fashion, city officials had little idea how to handle it. I, too, was breaking with tradition—balancing a yearning for a bygone childhood and the curiosity and wonderment that came with an entirely unsympathetic re-imagining of Christmas in a foreign land.

We were an unlikely bunch of foreigners to be holiday ambassadors. With at least two atheists/agnostics, a couple of Jews, and only one dedicated Christian, we may not have all had the most traditional Christmas upbringing, but all of us save for Tyra had celebrated it in one way or another.

In the days leading up to Christmas, Dylan, Jerry, and Grant—the three other male teachers—and I decided to make a trip to Beijing for a sort-of "boys' weekend out." On the ramshackle 12-hour night train from Taigu, we were fortunate to get a private four-bunk soft sleeper cabin, meaning that we could hold a conversation in relative comfort, perch on the second-story of adjacent bunk-beds, and take swigs of beer from giant glass bottles. While the rest of the train went dark at 10:00 PM, we had "lights out" at our own discretion.

Going to Beijing was like reaching the Promised Land in many ways—

familiar food, people who spoke English, and a constant stream of events and things to do. Almost without fail though, on every overnight train ride back to Taigu, a familiar feeling would creep in. As the swell of skyscrapers and high-rises fell away, it was like going back home to Brooklyn after Christmas with my cousins—the feeling that my life was in some way worse than all that I had experienced, that it wasn't good enough.

China, as a secular country, does not celebrate Christmas—at least, not in the way your average Christian family did in America—complete with midnight mass on Christmas Eve and the life-sized Jesus-in-the-manger nativity displays arranged alongside blow-up reindeer as front lawn decorations. What China does do to celebrate Christmas is shop, though even that is different than in America too. KFC capitalized on that well, with targeted advertisements that paired a family's consumption of a bucket of fried chicken with sledding and making snowmen on a blustery winter's day—all traditions that are not native to China. As night fell on my first day in Beijing, the four of us found ourselves at a divey Japanese restaurant. It epitomized, for me, the height of cultural confusion; everything about the situation seemed off.

For one thing, "Jingle Bells" was blaring on loop from the overhead speakers—literally, the first Christmas song I had heard all year—and the interior was decked out in wreaths, ornaments, bows, and other decorations, hanging from below the oversized menus and scattered around the check-out counters. Even the women behind the cash registers were wearing Santa hats to match their red-and-white aprons.

I couldn't help feeling like an outlier—a traitor to my family to whom I hadn't spoken in weeks, or more generally, to the country that I had—if not for good, then at least for the time being—left behind. In the same way that I wanted to be a good cultural ambassador of America to China, I also wanted to be a representative embodiment of America to my future family. How would I reconcile the part of me that waited in a lonely apartment in rural China on Christmas Eve knowing full well that there wouldn't be anything to greet me in the morning—no iconic Christmas specials, no gathering of presents around a tree, no baking chestnuts in the oven, no twinkle of Santa's sleigh passing across the night sky?

As the entrees were being served, I asked Darren and Jerry: "Isn't there something weird about those incredibly rare instances in life when all of your expectations are fulfilled, but yet you still don't feel satisfied?"

It was the first time any of us had had sushi in close to a year, and we were devouring the delicate rolls like newly released inmates. They both nodded, assuring me that the feeling was natural.

Compared to Beijing, Christmas in Taigu wasn't nearly as elaborate an affair. There were few reminders that it was even a holiday at all, save for the tiny windowsill effigies of Santa Claus and the handful of decorated fake trees at restaurant entrances that worked to drum up business. It was said that most of the recycled PVC plastic that went into making fake trees came from China, so it should have been no surprise that they were everywhere.

Many Chinese took Christmas to be the equivalent of Chinese New Year on the mainland—a traditional and reverent holiday spent doing things together with family. With the emphasis on togetherness, everyone I talked to was shocked when I revealed that I wouldn't be going home for the holidays. When I said it was about money, most scoffed, unable to see the connection with cost when there was an innate obligation to one's family.

"Won't your parents miss you?" students asked me, in between mouthfuls of braised pork and garlic shoots at our end-of-year banquets.

"Probably," I said, noncommittally, just before we toasted to the end of the first semester and the new year to come.

Holding true to our tradition from the previous year, we decided to cook a big meal together and eat it in the spacious, friendly comfort of Jerry's living room. A couple of our students, guessing our whereabouts, bombarded us with apples, a tradition on Christmas Eve in China, presumably because its name, *pingan jie,* shares the same first character with the Chinese word for apple (*pingguo*). Some of the apples were wrapped in colorful foil, others in individual boxes, some were dipped in various candied lacquers, and still more, were engraved and carved with designs.

For dinner on Christmas Eve, we decided to cook Mexican food, since Jerry and Grant had bought taco seasoning on a recent trip to Shanghai and we didn't know when else we would use it. Cooking dinner came to mean nearly as much fun and revelry as the eating itself. Each of us was responsible for different parts of the meal: Grant made the salsa, Jerry seasoned the meat, Dylan made tortillas, Tyra and Raina baked cookies from scratch, and I prepared the vegetables and rice. We ate and drank merrily, all to a playlist filled with equal parts Wham!, The Ventures, and Mariah Carey. I was reminded of the swine flu crisis in my first year, and how being cooped up together for so long made us stronger and more united as a group.

We had all drawn Secret Santa recipients. Some people had had enough foresight to buy their gifts during our trip to Beijing, but I led a second group on a trek out to the Walmart in Taiyuan for those of us who hadn't. Though our own families all had different traditions on when exactly to open gifts, we decided that Christmas Eve was as good a time as any, so after dinner and clean-up, we divvied out our presents and relished the slow afterglow of the holiday spirit. After that came the tradition to end all traditions—watching *A Charlie Brown Christmas* around Jerry's oversized computer monitor. I imagined myself as Charlie Brown—the slightly pathetic, but good-intentioned protagonist who seemed to get blamed more for society's failures than for its triumphs, but who took it upon himself to care for and support the group just the same.

After dinner, we decided to open up the sky lantern package that one of my students had given me as a Christmas gift and instructed that it would be most fortuitous to fly it on Christmas Eve. It was a remarkably simple contraption— basically a huge sheet of paper fashioned around a metal frame that sat atop a square-sized piece of wax. The idea was that you wrote your wishes on the paper, lit the wax, and once the balloon was full of air, sent it up into the sky. Though, admittedly, the lantern was an environmental nightmare since it was impossible to know where the lantern would land, or if it would potentially set fire to anything, it was also an extremely romantic notion: a group of friends jotting down their hopes for the New Year and sending them off into the cool night air. At about 1:00 AM we walked to a small clearing bereft of trees and sent up our sky lantern, taken by the wind past the tops of houses, and eventually out of sight.

We woke up on Christmas morning not to a flurry of snow and residual holiday cheer, but to the harsh, dry coldness of Taigu. It was as biting cold as any day we had seen in Taigu that year—the kind of cold that made your hands hurt to leave them uncovered. I was coughing and my nose was running when I left my house to get lunch. I had spent the better part of the week getting over a cold, and the arid chill only compounded the misery I felt as I walked the shaky cobblestone steps out past my front door to the lop-sided dirt road of North Yard.

If I hadn't known any better, it could have been just another day in Taigu. SUVs and taxis rumbled across the narrow path, honking at the frigid pedestrians clustered on either side. I went to eat *baozi* for lunch, tender round buns stuffed with meat and scallions, at our usual place, across from the hair salon and three meters to the left of the intersection. Just as I was leaving, something caught my eye. On the floor, slightly obscured by lingering traces of dirt, I found an ornament, a modest red ribbon adorned with the stylized text "Merry Christmas," still in its original packaging. I dusted it off and cradled it in the crook of my elbow all the way back home. With no tree on which to hang it, I tacked it to my front door, as if atoning for the neglected Christmases of my youth.

BOXING, MARRIAGE

We came to see a fight. The advertisements fixed to concrete scaffolding and café windows all around Chiang Mai had it up in big, bold-faced font: *"AUTHENTIC THAI BOXING: THE WORLD'S MOST DEVASTATING MARTIAL ART."* On the poster were grainy black-and-white photographs of unsmiling, brawny Thai men, wearing nothing but compression shorts and gloves. Some were brandishing gold-plated belts slumped over their shoulders or around their waists. Others were immortalized in action poses—one man taking a kick straight to the midsection, another doing a diving punch off the ropes.

I had seen a handful of video clips online. Muay Thai, the national sport of Thailand, had been popularized well outside of Thailand, but there was something kitsch about seeing the real thing. To be sure, it wasn't the main reason why Tyra and I came to Thailand, but once there, I knew what I wanted to see—a raw, uninhibited brawl.

From our hotel on the northern fringes of the city, it was a winding, circuitous route to the Loi Kroh Boxing Stadium near the Night Bazaar. The woman at the guesthouse where we shelled out 400 *baht* (about thirteen dollars) for our tickets insisted that we arrive 30 minutes ahead of time, so after dinner, we bolted from the restaurant and flagged down a tuk-tuk off the street. The driver spoke passable English and looked to be in his late-twenties. He knew the stadium immediately and knew exactly how much we had paid for our seats. I suspected that he also knew exactly what we could expect from the show, though evidently we weren't curious enough to ask.

"The fight starts at 9:00," he said, checking his watch. "Why do you go so early?"

Tyra and I looked at each other from across the backseat.

"They told us to get there 30 minutes before," Tyra said. The driver snorted and laughed.

"They only say that so you can buy drinks and make talk with the lady—," he calmly replied, the last part of his sentence trailing off into the wind. The entire backseat was a thick piece of unfinished plywood that bent and warped every time the three-wheeled motorbike made a sharp turn. I furrowed my brow and made reluctant, *I-told-you-so* eyes at Tyra. The woman at the guesthouse had probably given her spiel to foreigners so many times that she started to believe it was actually in their best interest.

The tuk-tuk stopped at the front of a shabby industrial complex that looked more like a waste management depot than it did a boxing arena. Before we could even pay the driver or get out of the vehicle, we were surrounded by girls dressed in little more than bibs and denim cut-offs shoving promotional flyers at us through the window. The entire street was lined with them, so much so that it could have been a coordinated affair—like some national "prostitution appreciation parade." Tuk-tuks pulled up every two or three paces, giving way to a new swarm of hookers tripping over themselves to greet the foreign tourists.

At the door to the arena, there was another woman who checked our tickets and ushered us inside. The stadium was warm and humid, the same as it was out on the street. On either side of the long hallway were shops and restaurants, and I noted the paper lanterns and neon-colored lights, the signs that hung in the windows that said Jenny's Happy Bar and The Eighth Dwarf, in curvy, stylized script. On sparse bar stools strewn out in front of the stores sat yet more girls, giving narrow glances and pouty lips to passing gentlemen in suit jackets and ties. They each had their legs crossed tightly under their skirts, like they were keeping a secret.

The usher turned to us and said that while we waited for the fight, we could help ourselves to drinks or food from the bar. It was like clockwork.

"Guinness, Heineken, Budweiser, anything you want," she said, as if she kept them on a running list in her head. "Food too—chicken wings, steak, mozzarella sticks." She paused carefully over each one to focus on the pronunciation. There was no mention of anything Thai. We both nodded our heads and kept walking. Then her voice got low and muffled. "Maybe after the show," she started in, looking at me. "You can ask for some other things too." A coy smirk passed over her lips. I gave her a look like maybe she should stop. Disappointed, she straightened up and turned to Tyra. "If that's something you both want, of course."

She sat us down in the first row. When we bought our tickets, the woman at the guesthouse said that regular seating cost 400 *baht* and VIP seating was 600. There was absolutely no distinction at the stadium, so I chalked it up in my mind to a sort-of "foreigner tax" for the gullible. I knew that wherever you traveled, local businesses charged different prices for the same things. They were all over-priced, but some more so than others—it was just a matter of shopping around and hoping that you got less ripped off than the person next to you.

The stadium was nothing like I had imagined it. Compared with major sports arenas in the states, it was laughable, a one-story compound with only a few shoddy banners and streamers decorating the path. The actual boxing ring was little more than a raised square platform in a circular pavilion, on which about a hundred stray collapsible rattan chairs lined all four sides. In front of them were these patio tables with mismatched tablecloths that didn't fit at all with the aesthetic.

At each table there was a sheet of paper with the words "Fight List" at the top that had the program for the night. I scanned the names of the combatants and the chronology of the smaller bit events that led up to the Big Fight. It was then that I started to get suspicious. On the right-hand column next to the names was a list of weights. The first sparring couple weighed in at 100 pounds and the next few proceeded in roughly eight-pound increments up to 132 pounds. At first I thought that they had printed the English wrong and they had meant to write kilograms instead of pounds. If not, I weighed 40 pounds more than the heaviest boxer and nearly doubled the weight of the lightest. Then, the sad truth of it hit me all at once: *The numbers were right—we had come to watch kids fight.*

The first combatants wore elaborately woven wreaths around their foreheads and carried small bundles of sage. They walked around the ring with the burning sage in their hands, cleansing the space. Next, they got down on their knees and began praying to each corner of the ring where a big, stalwart blocking pad with a fading "Jack Daniel's" logo was set up to absorb impact. Their heads touched the floor in front of them three times before they got to their feet, casually slid past their opponent, and repeated the ritual. I thought that it was an effort to beseech the gods for safety, to hope that whatever damage done wasn't permanent. With the wreaths wrapped around their heads, they almost looked like angels.

The boys took off the thick cloaks that were draped over their shoulders, and I saw their shirtless bodies for the first time. Their abdomens were finely sculpted, but they looked small and scared in the middle of the ring, despite the fact that the stadium was still largely empty. Their bulky gloves looked too big for their bodies, and their faces looked serious and worn, hardened by a childhood marred by strenuous training. I heard that young boys training to be pros had their stomachs lashed repeatedly with a broom until the nerve endings died, so they would not be able to feel the force of their opponent's punches.

The moment that Ruk Yom landed his first punch, I felt an inexorable sinking feeling in the pit of my gut. He was dressed in red shorts and gloves and the instant the bell clanged and the referee announced the start of the match, it was as if he had transformed into another person. Namwaan, his opponent in blue, was doomed nearly from the start. He was too tentative with his kicks and too slow to react. Ruk Yom had him up against the ropes, and, he tore into Namwaan, rounding punch after punch against his chest and head.

I could hardly believe what I was witnessing. It looked like a fight that could have taken place in a backyard or a school playground. I was half-expecting a parent or a teacher to swoop in and put an end to it at any minute. Instead, I had to wait for Namwaan to collapse into a heap on the floor and the referee to shout numbers over his prone body. The bell sounded again. The referee helped Namwaan shakily to his feet. He raised Ruk Yom's tiny arm triumphantly. The two fighters bowed to each other and exited the ring. The fight had lasted 43 seconds.

After the match, I turned to face Tyra. She looked the way I imagined I felt—her eyes were puffy and she was hunched over breathlessly in her chair, like she had just seen a car crash.

"I'm going to need a drink," Tyra said. She stood up from the chair and made a beeline for the bar. At the bar directly behind our rattan chairs, there was a red velvet love seat next to a pool table and a small dartboard. On the love seat were a gaggle of thinly dressed women wearing corsets and thigh-high stockings. In the middle, almost shielded from view, was a plump, balding man with a briefcase tucked between his large calves. As I watched, all four of the girls giggled and took turns touching the top of his gleaming, white head. Their hands were large and clumsy.

Tyra came back from the bar with a light-green slush topped with a pineapple rind and a lopsided parasol.

"I didn't even have to pay for this one," she said with a smile. "One of the bartenders up there must really like me." I turned around to find an unusually tall woman in a shimmery sequin top waving and blowing kisses in our direction.

"Do you find anything strange about the women here," I asked finally, still looking behind me.

"If by that you mean that they're not exactly women, then yes," she said, taking a sip from her drink. I jolted back around in my chair.

"They're all men—well, they were all *born* men." She took another sip. "Kathoeys, you know, ladyboys. Just look at their Adam's apples; it's really easy to tell."

It was true. The signs should have been painfully obvious—the over-the-top make-up, the lack of hips, the large busts, the deep voices. I looked all around the circular pavilion and for every bar it was the same—kathoeys on bar stools trying to seduce anyone in their path. I half-wondered if the men they attracted actually knew that they were ladyboys or just didn't care. I looked back to the ring at the new set of boxers getting ready to spar.

The next three matches passed with relative speed. They were still hard to watch, but the boys fighting were slightly older than the first pair, and I guess Tyra and I were both becoming desensitized. The matches were longer and they got increasingly more dramatic. Each time the bell rung to signal the end of a round, both combatants were rushed to their corners where a trainer sat them down on a chair in a squat metal basin and vigorously pounded and massaged their legs and back. They were each fed water from a narrow carafe through a straw and had their bodies doused with oils. After a time, the bell rang again and they had to duke it out for another five minute round.

My nerves tensed up, and my body grew stiff. I thought back to watching professional wrestling as a kid—the highly polished soap opera for boys and young men. I had always found it wildly entertaining. It was fun to see the new situations contrived for each of the characters week after week. I remembered something I heard a friend say about pro wrestling—that of course the whole thing was staged, but the real talent wasn't in the guy who was winning, but the guy simulating losing, and knowing that the winner was nothing without him. Thai boxing didn't have the same rules, but it still made sense—one boxer was powerless without the other.

Just before the Big Fight was what the program called a "Lady Fight." Two Thai women wearing sports bras and baggy shorts entered the ring and touched gloves in the center. They each had short, cropped hair and bulging biceps. After they left, a handful of the ladyboys rushed the stage to give a cabaret performance. Like the others hanging out in front of the bars, they were all wearing these ridiculous outfits that drew attention to their more feminine attributes. They were all Thai, but each wore a red sash with the name of a different country on it—Germany, China,

Italy. Then, one of the older ones crooned some song in Thai in the background while the rest of them danced. The dancing wasn't particularly good, but it was impossible to look away. Tyra grabbed my arm and pointed discreetly to the one wearing a Switzerland sash.

"Look, you can totally see that girl's nipple." I squinted and saw a flash of pink riding up over the top of her black tube top.

"Do you think they're fake?"

"If those breasts were real, you would be able to feel a shirt slipping down like that."

I had to agree. Her breasts were impossibly large, and perky. I sneaked a glance at Tyra for comparison. *Yes, unmistakably fake.* But there was still a part of me that deigned desperately to know what they felt like, to want them pushed up against my bare chest or have my face buried between them and never come out. I thought about Switzerland being fully naked in front of me, and how that would make me feel.

By the last fight, the sparsely populated arena finally filled up for the main attraction. The two boxers stood at the center of the ring and when the aging announcer signaled the start, the audience came to life with wild shouts and applause. Men dressed in long coats and crooked hats were making their way around the perimeter of the ring soliciting bets. The local Thais were in full force now and many of them flooded the stage to get up close to the fight. When one of the boxers had the other in a headlock, they started screaming in Thai, expressing either their approval or seething hate. Some pounded on the platform or banged on the ropes during the interludes between rounds, demanding that the boxer do better, that he do everything in his power to beat the other man.

The match lasted seven rounds, which was by far the longest of the night. Both boxers were visibly worn down and exhausted by the end when Sakeddao connected on a hulking uppercut to Hern Fah that sent him immediately on his back. There was a massive, bloody gash that surrounded his right eye and a mess of purple was trickling down his face. Again, the referee started shouting numbers, but Hern Fah wasn't moving at all. Eventually the bell rang and concerned trainers rushed up onto the platform. I peered over from my seat. He was breathing but still unconscious. The announcer wearily called the final results. People who lost money threw down their cups and headed for the exits.

After the fight was over, there was a mass exodus from the arena. Outside, a long queue of tuk-tuks had formed to take exhausted tourists back to their hotels. Tyra and I were among the last ones out, and the pick of tuk-tuks had already been whittled down to a paltry few. We announced the name of our hotel, and one man shouted a price. We went back and forth negotiating for a time, but finally we agreed on a number and crawled into the backseat. The driver was an older man, but I couldn't quite place his age. He looked like one of those guys who had been at his job for years.

The driver was wearing a knit hat and a sheepskin sweater buttoned all the way down to his waist. There were afghan throw rugs that covered the hard benches, and he had put plastic covering down on either side to prevent the drafty night wind from rushing through the windows. He had a square portrait of the king dangling from his rearview mirror. It was the same exact print we had seen in every train station, hotel, and convenience store in the country. He had a small altar set up on his dashboard with a rounded, oval container and a few sticks of lit incense. I saw his eyes perk up in the mirror.

"How did you like the show," he asked with a grin.

"It was really interesting," Tyra said, choosing her words carefully. "I didn't think they would be so young."

"The young ones, they play for the tourists," he said, in slightly broken English. "They fight for pride."

"Pride?" I asked confused, making sure I heard him right.

"Pride, family, honor," the driver went on, as if to showcase his knowledge of English synonyms. "They want to make their parents proud by winning."

I thought about how strange a concept that was. I imagined that if I were a parent, I would be terrified to watch my son get pummeled against the ropes, and ashamed that I was utterly powerless to help.

"How long you two will be here?"

"Only one week," I said. "Then we're flying to Indonesia."

"Indonesia," he said, letting the place settle on his tongue. "Then this must be a long honeymoon."

Tyra and I each looked at each other, half-grinning and half-bemused, casually assessing who would pipe up to set the driver straight.

Tyra turned to face the rearview mirror. "Actually," she started, a hint of embarrassment in her tone. "We're just—"

"We just got married last year," I sputtered, cutting her off. It came out so quickly that it surprised both of us. The driver slapped his leg in excitement.

"That's wonderful news!" he said with a booming voice.

Tyra turned to me and seemed to mouth *really?* in a mixture of wry amusement and playful scolding. It was the same way she looked at me whenever we got introduced to a new cab driver or waitress in China. They would inevitably ask where we were from, and eventually I got so frustrated and bored that I would answer with places like Iceland and the Czech Republic. She used to tell me that I shouldn't impersonate people from other countries. But this time—in English and miles away from China—it somehow felt more innocent.

I checked the rearview mirror again and the driver looked deep in thought, like he was searching hard for his next question.

"Marriage," he said, a fleeting nostalgic tone to his voice. "It's a great feeling, isn't it?"

"It is, it is," I said, shooting beaming grins in Tyra's direction. She smiled back at me.

"Where did you get married?"

"New York," I said. "Just a small group of friends and family at a church." Tyra pouted at me. Neither of us was particularly religious.

"But most of the ceremony was held at this roof terrace next door." I looked over, but Tyra just stifled a laugh and shook her head. "Really beautiful, the whole thing." The driver smiled plaintively in the mirror.

"I got married twenty-five years ago," the driver said. "Right here in Chiang Mai."

"That's incredible," Tyra said. "Twenty-five years is a long time."

"It is," he continued. "We have four children—two boys and two girls. Now one of the boys just got married and there will be a grandchild soon." The driver sat back in his seat. "I can't wait. They make their parents very proud." There was a pause and the driver slowed to a stop at an intersection.

"How about you," he asked. "Any children?" Again Tyra and I looked at each other.

"I don't think—," I wanted to say, but Tyra started before I could speak.

"We have a son, just six months old," she said. She tossed her hair from side to side, pleased with her own spontaneity.

"Congratulations!" the driver crooned, even more excitedly than the last time.

"Thank you," she said. "He's staying with my parents now. We're just so happy to have him."

I shot Tyra an urgent, entreating stare that begged the question: *what-do-you-think-you're-doing?* She shrugged back. *Nothing,* she seemed to insinuate. She focused her energies on the rearview mirror. The driver revved on the gas, and we puttered back down the street.

"He's certainly a handful, that one," she said. "I just hope my mom isn't having too much trouble with him."

"They get even worse when they are older," the driver called back. "Three years old is the hardest."

"Three? I'm having a hard time now. You would know, though, right? I mean you've done all of this already."

"Four times," the driver cried. "And now grandkids."

"And now grandkids!" Tyra screamed back. She was dizzy with excitement.

We reached a bumpy patch in the road and we both put our hands under the bench for support. Tyra reached over to grab mine but I was feeling anxious and pulled away. *I am no one's father,* I kept thinking in my head. She straightened up in her chair and cocked her head at me.

"It was fine before, but can we just cut it out now," I whispered in a low voice. Tyra looked back at me quizzically.

"I'm just having fun," she said hotly. "Go with it." She turned back to the driver.

"So what would you say is the big secret to parenting?" she asked him brightly. "What advice do you have for new parents?"

The driver paused for a second to think. We were rounding Moonmuang Road; the hotel was just up ahead.

"Children need a lot of attention," he said. "So it's good to have the older ones look after the young ones."

"You mean like having siblings?" The driver nodded.

"So maybe another brother or sister?" Tyra laughed and threw her hands up in the air.

"I don't know, what do you say, Dad?" she turned and clapped me lightly on the shoulder, but I was staring intently out the window, not wanting to say a word.

We pulled up to the hotel and Tyra thanked the driver and paid our fare. The tuk-tuk sputtered exhaust and slowly rumbled out of sight. It had gotten late—the gate in front of the hotel door was locked and we had to use an extra key to let ourselves in. Wordlessly, we climbed the two flights of stairs to our room. I fumbled in my pockets for the key and unlocked the door. Tyra went to the bathroom, and I took off my sweatshirt and jeans and changed into a pair of worn, striped pajamas. I folded the day's outfit and arranged it neatly on top of my bag. I walked over to the edge of the bed and slumped my head in my heads. I heard the toilet flush, and Tyra opened the door.

"Are we going to talk about that," she asked, her voice breaking the silence.

"What," I replied dumbly.

"You going all silent on me," she said indignantly. "What was that about?" I let the hum of her words fill the air for a moment.

"I don't know," I said, staring up at the ceiling. "I just can't think about children right now, that's all." Tyra flopped down onto the bed.

"I can't either, but I still like the *idea* of kids," she said back. "I mean, I want to have them someday." She looked a little surprised herself, as if the thought had just come to her for the first time.

"Can we talk about it in the morning," I asked, covering myself with the blanket. "It's getting late."

Tyra sighed and started to get undressed. She pulled her shirt over her head and turned to face the wall. She unclasped her bra and I saw the sharp outline of her breasts reflected in her shadow. I wondered how those kathoey men reacted to having breasts for the first time—how long it took to get used to them.

Tyra changed into an oversized t-shirt and hopped up onto the mattress.

"You know, that whole thing was your idea," she said, still a little annoyed. "I was just playing along." She slid into bed next to me and draped my arm reluctantly over hers.

I buried my head in the pillow. I knew that she was right, but I couldn't place why I had gotten angry. There was just something unsettling about what she said—about bringing children into this world.

ACCEPTANCE

Now in stride, you begin to reap the benefits of all your hard work. Your life is filled mostly with stability and a sense of belonging, of knowing your world. You will probably have one or two good friends. You will be familiar with the life of the campus and with the classroom. Now you can probably penetrate to the heart of what you want to get out of your experience.

BLACKOUT

In non-coastal cities in America, area blackouts are about as common as getting struck by lightning or becoming infected by West Nile Virus. They're so rare even that the simple mention of a date and place can often conjure up memories of an exact moment in a person's life.

In Taigu, area blackouts occurred about as frequently as trips to the dry cleaners or paying a utility bill. Rare was it that a few weeks passed without our breakers going haywire and the school losing power to one half of campus or the other. If we were lucky, we were spared the wrath that propelled convenience stores and student dorms on the north side into total darkness, but just as often, it was the paths and streetlamps that lined our locality that turned off and our houses that went dim. Sometimes that loss of power was just for a few hours, and at other times, for a day or more. Blackouts, especially in the evening, found us in one of two situations: either going to sleep early for lack of things to do, or attempting to offset our boredom with what was at our disposal—board games, a few candles, and a case of beer.

It was about 7:00 PM on one of these occasions, still early enough in the spring to be able to sit in the living room with the front door open and the blinds drawn and subsist on the modest amount of light that was coming through the windows. Jerry and Dylan came over and the three of us were making small talk in the living room, hoping that the situation wouldn't last. Eventually, Grant's laptop gave out and he, too, abandoned the privacy of his dark room and joined us. It was a scene oddly reminiscent of the front stoops outside of brownstones in my neighborhood back home. Sensing that it was getting dark, we began to make preparations.

"Anything new and exciting in class?" Dylan asked, as he cleared off the coffee table.

"We were playing Pictionary yesterday," Jerry started, "and one of my English majors kept drawing this blank circle with two eyes for the word 'aunt.'" He mimicked the expression with his own face. "God, it was hilarious."

"I've got them working on adaptations of Greek myths for their final," said Grant. "Oedipus and Thebes, Jason and the Argonauts, that kind of thing." It was just like Grant to teach Chinese students English by having them learn Greek myths.

With the exception of Jerry who opted to give written final exams, we all decided to administer oral skits as the end of the year grade assessment. Our bosses only really cared that we had some sort of final to close out the year, but never specified exactly what kind. I split my students into groups of four and had them mull over a hypothetical worst-case scenario: *You and your group-mates are high up in a hot air balloon and notice that it has begun to leak. What do you do?*

Each group would have fifteen minutes to perform their skits in front of the class and I would be meeting individually with each one to check the script for errors and plagiarism. I usually tolerated copying in the first draft so long as they changed it by the time of their performance. But despite my tireless soapboxing, students never seemed to fully grasp the American gravity of plagiarism. Worse still, though, was the handful of students who attended less than one or two classes all year, but who were convinced that they were entitled to a passing grade. In spite of it being an oral English class, most of those students could neither speak nor understand the simplest of phrases.

During my first semester, it was less of a problem: the H1N1 epidemic put the campus on lock-down for two straight months. I forgave students who used it as an excuse for not being able to return to school, whether or not I believed them. But since then, there had been no such calamity. Attendance for all of my classes dropped by almost half, and those who rarely came before stopped coming altogether.

Disheartened and frustrated, I warned my students that those who didn't start regularly attending class would receive a zero for their final grade. For the first week following my announcement, attendance spiked, but it wasn't long before it began to fall again. As a last resort, I instituted a cap for attendance: those who had attended less than twenty percent of my classes all year—a remarkably minimal requirement considering that attendance was the crux of my grading rubric—would not be allowed to take the final exam.

I didn't think there would be much, if any, pushback from my students. Surely those who had never come to class and who had never handed in a single homework assignment knew that they would be failing. I had laid out all of the class guidelines at the beginning of the semester. But I had forgotten an unwritten rule of the Chinese educational system: that passing the final exam means passing the class, regardless of attendance record.

When suddenly I wrenched that single chance from their hands, students were forced to confront a much graver predicament. Begrudgingly, they returned to class, with a mix of shock, embarrassment, hostility, and desperation. Having explained my rationale again and again, each time with another third of the class watching, I thought I had finally put the issue to rest.

But like the blackouts that wreaked unforeseen havoc on my living quarters, so too did that subset of students who, one after the other, appeared uninvited at my house to discuss the matter. Both the blackouts and the student visits seemed to be governed entirely by the tides of chance. Students dropped by at all hours of the day and evening, most bearing gifts, or the promise of future gifts—a lavish dinner, a trip to the massage parlor, beautiful girls at a nightclub. One came with a "translator"— one of the better students in the same class—and another with a Chinese friend of mine who thought he could use that relationship with me to improve his grade.

I surprised myself by my own lack of sympathy. Without coming to class, there was no way to have learned anything that I taught, so what could they possibly contribute to the exam? I got all kinds of excuses for missing class—full-time jobs in other cities, experiments that lasted for months. I told them that if they could explain to me in English why they thought they deserved the chance to take the exam, I would let them take it. None of them did.

Where it would have been much easier to give in, I stayed firm. I lied at first, saying that it was a rule my boss had imposed, then finally owned up to it myself. I wanted to teach them a lesson that I felt as graduate students they should have learned a long time ago. It wasn't long before word spread and students in other classes found out. Then even they tried to petition for their struggling classmates—pleading with their own foreign teachers to get me to change my mind. But my decision was final.

My goal as a teacher was to reward effort. It didn't bother me if a student's English level was not high so long as he or she made some kind of an effort to improve—coming to class, following the lesson, asking questions if he or she didn't understand. My only hope was that the student's English level at the end of a semester was better than where it started. It was clear from current performance, as well as looking at the grades from the past semester, that this wasn't the case for these students. But all the while, I was beginning to doubt myself.

On the day of the blackout, I had already sunk into my own well of self-pity. Grant caught me shirtless in my room, lying sprawled out on my bed and listening to

Habib Koité at the highest volume my speakers could reach, the swoops and crashes of the Malian drum beats washing over my body like waves. I told him that I wanted to cleanse my entire being, as if this otherworldly music could burn off my skin and regenerate it anew.

I was devastated by the belief that I had ruined these students' lives—that because of the stubbornness of my own principles, their paths could be irreparably changed for the worse. They had grown up in a different culture and with a different education system than I, so perhaps it wasn't fair that I was subjecting them to something so utterly foreign.

As it got close to the time when we would have to start lighting candles, there came a rap at my screen door. By then the room was filled with a soft pale glow and the objects and the three other faces were hardly distinguishable from one another, accented only by occasional movement. But I immediately recognized the figure at my door as my student, Susan. Unlike my other flunkouts, during the previous semester she had performed at the top of her class, but this spring I had seen her only a few times. Despite my esteem for her as a student, I had an obligation to be fair. I asked her friends in class to tell her that due to her absences, she would not be allowed to take the final exam.

She came to my house alone as a single, hunched silhouette in the doorframe. Like most girls at the university, she wore plain clothes, no make-up, and kept her hair in a simple ponytail. Outside, the sun had set, and already a grainy fog was filling in the sky. She carried a bundle of bananas—a bribe of sorts, but one that somehow felt more genuine than most. Her eyes would hardly meet mine at first—oscillating between her shoes and the horizon in the distance behind my house. Despite my invitation to come in, she preferred to keep her distance.

She began to explain the reasons for her disappearance from class. I was surprised by the degree to which she could still make herself understood in English, despite the long hiatus.

"A few months ago, I found out that I was pregnant," she said calmly, like she were setting out clothes on a line to dry. Her eyes darted quickly to her enlarged midsection. "But at that time, my boyfriend and I were still single."

Her boyfriend was the same year and major that she was in school. Susan motioned to Grant still sitting on the couch. "One of his students," she said, though none of the guys were paying attention. A child out of wedlock in China was cause for scandal, so her parents wanted a marriage, but that still wouldn't solve the issue of the baby.

"We talked a lot about what we should do," Susan continued. Her speech started slowly, then grew fast like a confession. On the one hand, abortion was a relatively cheap and easy solution, but with it came a host of moral dilemmas.

"My parents are farmers," she said, "and are very traditional. So, finally we decided to keep it," she said. "To bring the baby into the world." Not long after, her parents made preparations for the wedding. Everyone involved—her boyfriend included—was amazingly obliging throughout, but all the details about the pregnancy were kept private.

Susan and her boyfriend were wedded back in their hometown, a small ceremony with just their closest friends and family. Following that, she returned back to school, and began briefly attending class again—a story that checked out with my own attendance records.

"When I came back, I thought everything would be normal," Susan went on. "But my classmates didn't want to talk to me anymore. Everyone noticed my stomach. They said I was like a different person." There were other complications from the pregnancy too—waking up feeling sick every morning, wanting to throw up. She turned her body away from the door, like she was ashamed of it.

"My parents wanted me to return home and not come back to school," she said. Her voice got low and raspy. Not knowing what else to do, she agreed.

By now, the night sky was cascading across her face. Activity along the small bypaths outside my house had slowed to a crawl. I could tell by the creases in her eyes that Susan was on the brink of tears. This was an incredibly embarrassing thing to admit to anyone—particularly a foreign English teacher. She told me she would be taking the next year off from school in order to give birth, and afterward, she might not come back to finish her degree. I speculated that very few people knew the full extent of her predicament.

I could only think of one question: "Why now?"

She explained, "I wanted to tell you earlier. I just didn't know how."

As I looked out at the swirl of gray and black behind her, the entire scope of human experience became clear to me for a single instant. Just one year earlier, she was a child. Now standing before me she was a mother-to-be, four-months pregnant, waiting for me to hand down my judgment. She was just barely older than I but looked years younger. I could only think of her in class. Susan in the fourth row. Susan in the stretchy dress, hands clasped around her stomach like a life preserver. She was the first pregnant person my age that I had ever met. Given the right circumstances, it could have happened to any one of us. I took a long breath before responding

"Okay," I told her. "You can take the exam."

SAND

My ass was sore for a week. Overnight train rides were spent on my stomach, meals were taken over the backs of chairs, and I was more comfortable than ever about squatting over toilets. It was probably how long the damn thing took. I don't care who you are: three hours on the back of a camel will do strange things to your body.

Tyra and I saw brochures for the outing at our hostel in western Gansu Province. The literature was picketed with phrases like "relive the mystery of the Silk Road" and "experience one thousand and one Arabian nights!"; though the translations weren't nearly as polished. But what really sold us were the tiny snapshots superimposed over the text—smiling tourists posing on camelback, peeking out from inside tents, and climbing up the immaculate sandbanks. "Almost two full days in the beautiful Mingsha Sand Dunes," the advertisement continued, "complete with an overnight stay in the desert followed by a breathtaking morning sunrise!"

There were seven of us on the trip: two other couples, one Chinese and one American, and an outgoing twenty-six-year-old from Shanghai, intent on seeing more of her own country. She was the third in the camel caravan behind me and Tyra, followed by the two couples. An eighth camel, charged with carrying the camping tents and cooking supplies, brought up the rear.

Each camel was tied to the one in front of it with a thick rope, a wad of knotted string protruding through its nostril and capped with a stopper to hold it in place. Any hold-up in the journey meant that each subsequent camel was turned sideways, its head precariously hooked to the one behind, forcing the camels to quickly learn to move in tandem. At the head of the caravan was an older Chinese gentleman of either Tibetan or Uighur descent whose inhabitants were not uncommon in the Far West.

The older gentleman acted as the foreman, and walked the end of the rope out in front of the line of camels; for a man of fifty or sixty, he was rugged and fit. It was the middle of July, and the desert was sweltering. The foreman was wearing a long-sleeve shirt, gloves, and a hat to protect himself from the sun. By contrast, I had rolled up the sleeves of my thin T-shirt to my shoulders and was tugging helplessly at the hem of my jeans. Tyra was wearing black leggings and a button-down shirt and looked about as flustered as I.

It didn't take long before I began to tire of the camel ride. Out in the dunes, everything started to look the same: on all sides there were white clouds, blue skies, and towering piles of sand that seemed to reach the stratosphere. The size and scale of it was dizzying. The closest I had ever come to sand was the gravelly Coney Island coast; even in memory, that bore almost no resemblance to the endless, shimmering mounds that swelled and swooped around me now.

I could tell Tyra was exhausted—she didn't say a single word as we bobbed up and down through the desert. Still, it was easy to be entertained by the back-and-forth between the foreman and the young, unmarried Chinese woman. She wanted to know everything about his life—when he started raising camels, how much he made per year, what his family was like. It appeared that the Chinese fascination for *otherness* extended well beyond the American foreigner, to its marginalized citizenry as well.

The foreman responded to every nagging inquiry. The camels were not his, he explained, but he was able to rent them from a friend to do his treks. His expertise was in leading trips out to the desert and the care with which he took to make his foreign guests comfortable. He had been doing it for over thirty years, and in the winters when it got too cold to camp in the desert overnight, he helped raise his grandchildren at home, of which he had over a dozen.

The woman was intrigued. "How do you make your foreign guests comfortable if you can't speak any English?" she asked with a smirk. Conversation up to that point had been entirely in Chinese. The foreman remained unfazed.

"Once a foreigner asked me where he could go to the bathroom," he recalled, repeating the word "bathroom" in English. He hadn't understood what the word meant and asked the tourist to repeat the question.

"Toilet," the Australian pleaded, looking close to desperation. "Where can I find the toilet?"

The foreman smiled. He pointed to a shrub in the distance and, in his most exaggerated English, shouted, "There is toilet." The whole caravan chuckled in unison.

"So besides speaking English," the woman asked snidely, "what else can you do?" The foreman thought for a moment.

"I can sing," he exclaimed, and launched into an enthusiastic rendition of a popular Chinese folk song. The woman clapped her hands and looked pleased.

"What about you?"

"I don't sing," the woman said dismissively, waving a hand in front of her face.

"Well I'm not going to sing alone," said the foreman. "You there," he said looking up at me, the first one in line. "How about it?"

"Me?" I asked defensively, surprised to be singled out. "I can't sing either." The foreman shook his head.

"Oh I'm sure you can sing," he said eagerly. "All you Americans must be able to sing something. What about your national anthem?"

There were few things I detested more than my own singing voice. Karaoke with friends in an enclosed room was one thing, but the desert was suspiciously quiet and sound tends to carry for a long time across an open space. I spun around to look at Tyra. She was applying a new layer of sunscreen; the others on the tour looked even more uninterested.

"No, I'd really rather not," I said. I thought it was an adequate rejection.

"You need to sing," he paused, "or else I'm turning all of us around." He was staring me dead in the eyes.

"I don't want to sing," I blurted out, half-shouting. The foreman's pace slowed to a halt. The only sound was the light crunch of sand beneath my camel's hooves. No one said anything for what felt like minutes, and then, at last, the woman from Shanghai piped up.

"What else can you do?" she asked him. The foreman scratched his head.

"I can cook," he said, gradually taking the reins in his hand and resumed course.

At some point along the way I managed to fall asleep. To fall asleep riding on the back of a moving camel sounds hyperbolic, but there is something unique about the experience. I could almost picture myself a wealthy Chinese merchant, a team of vassals at my beck-and-call, lazily slouching along the Silk Road; for the moment, neither time nor bodily desires was of the least concern.

When we stopped it was almost dark. The foreman helped let us down and began unpacking the tents and cooking equipment. He tied the first camel to the last, rigging them in a closed loop, and instructed each one to kneel on the ground one by one. He announced that we would have dinner there at the base in an hour, but that in the meantime, we should enjoy the sunset on the lookout of a tall, sandy peak he pointed to not far in the distance.

From the moment I stepped off the camel, I was running across the plains, rolling down hills, and scrambling up embankments. I was six years old again playing in a giant, ever-expansive sandbox. Tyra, feeling my mood, began stalking me like a lion, and the two of us got down on all fours, pouncing and shuffling barefoot in our African Sahara. When she got close enough to touch, I wrestled her to the ground, dusting her clothes and mine with sand.

We tore our way up the sandy peak to the lookout. At one point, we tried to race headlong up the nearly vertical shaft, but with each beleaguered step, we slipped increasingly more deeply into sand, laughing and shrieking as we sank. When we reached the top, the lone Chinese woman offered to take our picture. Tyra and I sat with our backs to the sunset in the distance, her head nestled firmly in the crook of my neck.

The group gathered for dinner on two squat, collapsible tables back at base. The foreman had constructed a small fire out of packed twigs and brush. He brought out seven metal containers and placed them on the tables. Under each lid was a brick of instant noodles mixed with the once hot water transported from the town. On all accounts, it was a letdown. My body was starving, and after a full day in the desert sun, the last thing I wanted to eat was lukewarm noodles.

The foreman, sensing the collective disappointment, explained: "The government doesn't give me enough money to provide any food for the trip," he said, in his accented Mandarin. "But since I expect tourists not to bring enough, I buy this out of my own pocket."

The foreman looked around the circle but still strained to make eye contact with me. It was easy enough not to trust him, to imagine that he skimmed the extra money off the top to pay for cigarettes and liquor and gambling. But the narrative didn't seem to fit. I pulled a flimsy packaged sausage from my bag and added it to the water. It was something I almost never ate, but Tyra had packed it just in case. I slurped up my noodles in silence.

Nearby, the camels snorted and shifted positions. They slept a stone's throw away from where the foreman had set-up our sleeping tents. All roped together in a circle, they looked like this single living entity, the silhouette of their humps rising and falling with their breath. With no respite from the cold night air, nor any food or water of their own, they still seemed perfectly, dispassionately, content.

Pretty soon everyone began preparing for sleep. Each of the couples had their own tent, and the unmarried woman had one to herself. The foreman slept outside beneath the stars—"how he liked it"—though I suspected it was more that he preferred not to pay to rent an additional tent. The tents were roomy but provisions were scarce. Other than a thin mat, the only covering we had was the tattered fleece blanket we had previously used as a makeshift saddle on the camels.

I was unfolding the mat when Tyra grabbed my arm to stop me. She had changed into a loose-fitting dress that dipped well beneath her neck and rested just above her ankles. Her lips were a searing red, and she had a ferocious glint in her eye. She pointed at me, then at herself, and finally at the mesh flap of the tent leading outside. In her hand was the clear plastic bag of condoms we had been steadily exhausting throughout the trip. I nodded eagerly and she laughed, stashing the bag in her purse.

We made our move after the last of the tents went dark. Tyra brought the tiny flashlight we had used to examine cave paintings all morning, her purse, and the quick-dry travel towel we had been sharing, and we slogged up the little ridge. Our tiny encampment was positioned in a man-made ditch at the bottom of a hill, but there was higher ground to every side of us like the raised crust around a dessert's center. The sand kept giving underfoot. Each step had to be calculated, like we were snowshoeing up a steep cliff.

When we reached the top, Tyra pointed at the sky. I'd never seen stars like the ones that night; the constellations shined like stadium lights in the distance. Beyond the ridge's lip, the view was the same: hundreds of flecked sand dunes, the moonlight shimmering off their glittery surfaces like a theater packed with flashbulbs—an entire inter-stellar audience waiting for the curtain to be drawn and for the show to begin.

Tyra rolled out the towel and laid it gently over the sand, and I held her tightly, easing her body to the ground. She undid the buckle to my belt, and I carefully folded the tapered ends of her dress above her waist. All at once, a wave of fear came over me. Not two hours earlier, the sand was near scalding to the touch, but now it was cold, sending chills up my feet.

I was shaking. It felt like the stars were glaring down at me, fixing me with a dark force. In a parallel world, there would be no cosmic witnesses, no dull hum across the floating expanse—the shared moment existing for the two of us and us alone.

As quickly as I thought them, the words began to form in my mouth. "I don't—," I muttered under my breath, but just then something stirred inside me. A blast of wind rolled over the dune, fanning out the sand beneath Tyra. I grabbed her arms and held them firmly to the ground. Her body shook as the sand pulsed and swayed, each thrust sending the earth's force resisting back against us and into the wind.

Beads of sweat trickled down the nape of my neck, and when it was over, we were both still breathing heavily, Tyra on her back, and me crouched in front of her, the jeans still looped around my ankles. The sand had coursed through her hair and mine, matting it at obtuse angles. For some time, everything around us was still. She propped herself up with both arms and exhaled deeply into the sky—her blue eyes scanning the clouds like a beacon in the desert.

I dreamt that Tyra and I had gathered the towel and the clothes and ambled back down the ridge to our tent. I imagined us huddled close together on the thin mat—her back curving to form a tight seal against my chest, and my arms clasped firmly against hers.

But in the morning, we awoke to the startled, raspy bray of the foreman. He was standing downwind from the spot on the sand where we had inadvertently spent the night, his hands resting indignantly on his hips. We figured that after having seen our tent empty he went looking for us, and was surprised to see the two of us curled up on the towel, a wild tangle of clothes in a heap at our side.

"Pack up your things," he said with a grin, "and make it fast." He shook his head and turned back down the ditch to join the other couples and the lone woman from Shanghai. They were all watching the sunrise break over the crest of the horizon and fill in the hills and valleys of sand. Tyra turned to face me.

"That was dumb," she said, unabashed. She reached out and began pulling on articles of clothing. I sat bolt upright, my face red. I wrung my shirt over my head and quietly took Tyra's hand in mine. We both turned to look at the sunrise. It was like nothing either one of us could have imagined.

DANCE DANCE (CULTURAL) REVOLUTION

Before I came to China, I was terrified of dancing. The thought of priming my clumsy adolescent body to step in beat was enough to send shivers down my spine. An image of a flummoxed figure, gyrating wildly and making stabbing motions at the air was my impression of my own kinesthesia. I was panic-stricken at having to dance alone, but even more so at the primeval ritual of doing so with another person. I abhorred the adolescent phase of school dances, the coming together of girl and boy from opposing gymnasium walls, and I couldn't comprehend the appeal of a nightclub—a sardine sweat-box brimming with expectations as cloying and self-evident as a man's cologne.

When I first arrived in Taigu, I was told a lot about the dance parties that for years had been a permanent fixture at the foreign Fellow apartments. Teachers invited their friends and students for a cultural exchange of a non-academic and non-verbal nature. It gave Chinese friends the opportunity to experience a foreign party in spite of the limitations imposed by China, including the 11:00 PM student curfew that resulted in the ungodly early start time of 8:30. Because of floor damage incurred from previous dance parties at their own house, my co-Fellows Rachel and Nate insisted that the tradition of hosting such events—a sought after and noble post, they assured us—would fall to Grant and me.

I felt the way about dancing that I did about big, outrageous outings to Chinese KTV—I enjoyed them provided that I was aided by a lack of adequate lighting and a generous amount of alcohol. Unlike me, however, Grant had absolutely no qualms about dancing. He used to wake up every morning to the 80s mainstay "Safety Dance," and occasionally he would come into my room, the song still blaring from his speakers, and coax me out of bed with the power of song and dance. Most dance parties, he preferred being perfectly sober, and it was only if he wanted to goad Nate and Darren—or later, Jerry and Dylan—into testing their limits that he ever really got into trouble. People were always shocked at how his body moved—twisting and shaking all 210 pounds around like he was this unstoppable wrecking ball.

Beginning with that first weekend in September and continuing about twice a month for all two years of my Fellowship, Grant and I played host to dozens of dance parties, so many that we had even exacted the art of party preparation down to a science. First came the text message invitations in the afternoon, then the buying of alcohol after dinner, and finally, there was the setting up of the house itself. After queuing up "Layla" on the speakers in the living room (The Derek and the Dominoes original, it should be noted), we took out the trash, arranged the furniture, moved all unnecessary articles into Grant's room (jackets, desk lamps, house slippers), stocked the flimsy coffee table with beer cans and positioned it against my door to guard against intruders, and fired up the disco ball using the *Jurassic Park*-sized flashlight jury-rigged to our bookshelf.

By then the "Dance Party Warm-Up" playlist had already cycled through three more songs—Kanye West's "Slow Jamz," KT Tunstall's "Suddenly I See," and The Temptations' "Get Ready." By the time "The Seed (2.0)" by The Roots came on, the clock read 8:30 and the front door was propped open and ready for business. In cold weather, guests piled coats and sweaters on the couch, and in the spring, due to space constraints and incessant heat, the party spilled over to include the front porch. The living room was as hot as a cauldron regardless of the season, and there were typically 40 to 50 people who showed up at any given party. Each time the parties went off in exactly the same fashion, and in their own way, they always proved successful—that is to say, we never once had a dud.

At every dance party we ever threw in Taigu, I put myself in charge of music. It was not that I thought my taste was better than anyone else's, but none of the foreigners had strong feelings about DJing, and it was something that I really came to enjoy. With only a few people at the start, it was experimental hour—a time to audition potential songs before their prime-time debut. As the Chinese guests' interest in English songs waned, it was necessary to inject a dose of Chinese pop. A lot of high-energy songs in a row, and the mood was set for a slower-paced, cool down song. Regardless of what it was, if I played a song enough times, it started to become imbued with a certain significance. I enjoyed the feeling of playing God, of having the ability to influence people's emotions with the touch of a button.

During the party, I typically spent a third of the time dancing, a third doing damage control, and a third making sure I was back to the speakers with enough time to change songs. Early on, I used to have a tradition where at 10:00 all the males did push-ups on my linoleum kitchen floor before rushing out shirtless to the faint amusement of the living room mob. I kept a stash of outlandish hats and sunglasses on the coat rack that guests could try on and wear. In my last semester, I began taking informal break-dancing lessons from a student group at the university and sanctioned small ciphers as part of the dance party to practice new moves. As the person responsible for the execution of each party, I had an almost dictatorial grasp on how the evening's events unfolded—a power that I was unwilling to concede.

It took the innocence of Chinese dance parties for me to overcome my self-consciousness about dancing. There was no pressure to see or be seen, and, short of blowing out the speakers, we could really be as loud and rambunctious as we wanted. Our boss Xiao Yin, long ago wise to the uniquely American tradition, allowed us one night a week where the rules did not apply. If he got drunk enough after a banquet, he sometimes followed us home to take part himself. The dance parties were one of the few things that hardly changed from my first to my second year—which was in and of itself a great source of comfort.

To be sure, there was nothing particularly glamorous about the dance parties—glittery sequins were peeling off from the disco ball and the floor was glazed with a layer of dried beer. But the main reason that they had been so successful was that it was never hard to get friends to come. Most of the students at the university were so bored on a given Saturday night that any break from their prescribed routine of chatting online or studying in the library was a welcome respite. It was easy to entice them to a bizarre party hosted by foreigners. Getting them to dance, however, was another issue entirely.

Halfway through the spring semester, my first-year English majors told me that they would be organizing a dance party on the fourth floor of *guyuan*, the school cafeteria. It was to be held in a room outfitted with a large dancing space as well as a stage, special sound and lighting equipment, and a dedicated operator. They insisted that the party was in our honor—a way to thank us for a year's worth of teaching—but they didn't take our advice when it came to the execution. Instead of simply playing music and allowing people to dance, there would be a prescribed program—hosts, contests, breaks for song numbers, closing remarks. It was the Chinese approach to throwing a party. They asked if I could act as DJ, and I couldn't say no.

As soon as I consented, the other plans quickly fell into place. It was the first time we had used *guyuan* for a party, and I was excited to be projecting music to an audience four or five times the capacity that could fit in my living room. The English majors took care of all of the logistics that Grant and I usually had to handle—buying snacks and beer and setting up the space. But it was only until the day of the party—

after the invitations went out to the usual slew of party-goers and all of the supplies had been procured—that Mary and Lisa, the students in charge of organizing the event, informed us that the time had been changed. Instead of being from 7:30 to 10:00 (late by campus standards), it would now be happening from 6:00 to 8:00.

I was playing basketball with a few of my graduate students when Grant called about the change. He and one of my old students, Frank, had been singled out to be hosts for the evening's ceremonies. They were both effusive and lively and were cast perfectly for the roles. They planned to do a stand-up comedy routine in the style of Chinese crosstalk, where two players engage in a dialogue laced heavily with language puns and deliver it in a rapid, bantering style. Grant wrote the script for a take on the classic Abbott and Costello routine—except instead of baseball, they would make allusions to some of the key members of China's governing leadership.

It wasn't edgy enough for anyone to take offense. The punchline was a play on Chinese President Hu Jintao's name, which in English came out as, "Who (Hu) is the president of China?" Taigu, which could aptly be compared culturally and geographically to America's Midwest, tended to be far more conservative than those towns on the coast or some of the more cosmopolitan cities in southern China. That conservatism largely manifested itself in traditional values. People were by and large still wary of change, and very few openly questioned the government. It was what even young Beijing intellectuals may have called "backwards" thinking, to say nothing of critics in the West. With the exception of a new three-story mall, most of the town looked like it had remained unchanged since the early 1960s. Sometimes it felt to me that people's ideologies were rooted in that same period.

When I got the call from Grant, I was furious.

"How could you let this happen?" I asked him, breathing heavily into the phone. Even though I realized that it was nearly impossible for events to go off as planned in China, it still frustrated me to no end.

"It's the school," he said, trying to be diplomatic. "The students don't have any control over it." I was standing on the sidelines of the basketball court and my students were waiting for me to finish talking before starting the next game.

"What do you mean they don't have any control over it? Didn't they book the space in advance?"

"They did," Grant continued, "but the administration has some event they're using it for. They told the students they had to make the party earlier." There was a short pause on the phone, and the whole time I kept my eyes fixed to the ground so my students couldn't see my expression. "I'm not happy about it either."

According to the student organizers, school administrators had co-opted the space for a singing competition in honor of the Communist Party's 90th Anniversary. It hardly mattered that our students had reserved the space months in advance and were just being told of the change an hour before the event would go off: this was China, and plans changed at the drop of a hat. A restaurant abruptly closing, Chinese friends sent to work in other cities for months during the school year, travel plans shifting because of train tickets being sold out. China was ephemeral that way; it was hard to count on anything.

It turned out that I wasn't alone—the other teachers were also livid about the situation. There was no time to warn other students of the change, and what was worse—the real issue at stake—was who actually wanted to go to a dance party that started when the sun was still out? Most students would hardly be finished with dinner at that time. I was surprised at the nonchalance with which news like this always got communicated, how students never got angry or hostile about their lack of agency. The same was true of citizens and the government. In Chinese, there is an expression to "eat bitter," and people in the countryside embodied it better than most. I couldn't imagine the stalwart resolve necessary to actually affect lasting change.

I put the phone back in my pocket and turned to Jackie.

"I forgot, there are no human rights in China," I muttered in Mandarin, forgetting momentarily where I was. Jackie blinked twice at me, the basketball clasped between his hands. I could tell that he didn't quite know how to respond. I shook my head, waving off the comment—I didn't really know either.

Without any time to shower or eat dinner, I went straight from the basketball courts to the fourth floor of the cafeteria to help set up for the party. All of the other foreigners were in as cheerful and as conciliatory a mood as they could muster. Tyra had even managed to bring Raina—her roommate—to the party, a considerable feat given that Raina often preferred to engage in her own activities separate from the other teachers. Dylan, who wouldn't dance without alcohol, came in smelling of whiskey. Though he'd planned on being able to drink with us over dinner, he'd had to down a few shots alone in his room as a result of the time shift. I looked around the room at the dozen or so plastic-wrapped cases of beer; not one of them had been opened.

To my surprise, people arrived on time. Grant and Frank finished their crosstalk routine, and Mary, one of the event organizers, got on stage to make some opening remarks and announce the start of the party. She was wearing a long blue dress with rows of frills and ruffles like the tiers of a wedding cake. Both the dress and the tottering pair of high heels she wore made her look out of place at the front of the stage. No one ever dressed up for dance parties at my house unless we enforced a theme, but this had the vague flavor of a middle school dance, and students jumped at the opportunity to make an impression. The entire audience numbered no more than 40 people, sitting on chairs near the wall of the large space, looking like they had no intention of ever getting up.

When Mary was finished, it was my cue to start the music, and like clockwork, all of the foreigners sprang into action. We all jumped into the middle of the gigantic white-walled room and, with sunlight still bleeding through the windows, began pulling people off of walls and chairs in an attempt to get them to dance. Usually a generous amount of prodding and hand-holding was par for the course, but this was by far the most effort we had ever had to exert. We succeeded in roping in a few students, but the vast majority continued to stand and stare at us like we were aboriginals performing a kind of rain dance.

It was a far cry from the dance scene in Beijing where we sometimes spent long weekends. Sleek, modern, and outfitted with state-of-the art equipment, Beijing nightclubs seemed antithetical to the antiquated gray cafeteria with its checker-tiled floor and slate-and-brick ping pong tables that lay pushed up against the windows. There were overt sexual undertones there that were completely absent in the countryside. Dancing was its own form of cultural subversion, a rebellion against the more sanctioned forms of entertainment of which the government approved. Even in the big cities, it had always begun as a Western import, the very same model that we adapted and implemented for Taigu.

By 7:30, the dance party, much to my utter disbelief, was actually quite good. On word of mouth alone, we were able to get over 300 people to show up for the event—about the room's capacity. The sun had gone down and students were still streaming through the front doors. Strobe lights were cascading across the floor. I kept adjusting the playlist after each song, dancing for three or four minutes before returning back to the sound booth. The students, able to fade anonymously into the crowd, found the courage to start dancing. Soon, they grew eager for a piece of the spotlight. Theirs was a style half-mimicked from American music videos and half-appropriated from the foreign teachers themselves. The vast majority didn't give off the most favorable reflection—jumping and flopping around like fish out of water.

It was exactly at 8:00 when Mary gracefully returned to the stage and announced that the party was over. With a smile akin to that of a television news anchor, she thanked everyone for coming and did a curtsy in her blue dress.

"The next event will soon be starting," she said, "and it is best if you all swiftly find the exits and return to your dormitories."

I looked around, expecting most of the students to loiter haltingly in the room for a while, in no rush to leave the party. But almost immediately, students began packing up their things and heading for the exits. A handful thanked me on the way out, waving and smiling exuberantly as they bounded for the stairs. I rounded up a couple of them and in a segregated corner of the room, I began calling for resistance—a chance to stand up to the administration. But my students were mired in inaction. It felt like a holdover from the Cultural Revolution—people were too afraid to do anything but bend to the will of authority. After all, what was more important to them: a permanent black mark on their record or some stupid dance party?

I caught up with Mary as she was helping to put away the uneaten snacks and fold up some of the tables.

"Can you believe this?" I asked her, noticeably embittered. "The party's over just like that?" She looked at me cross-eyed, unsure what I meant. Then she pursed her lips and spoke with an apologetic tone.

"Oh, I'm so sorry," she said. "I thought the other teachers told you. The school needed to use the room for—"

"I know that," I said, a little too curt. "But why didn't we try to do something about it." Again, she fixed me with a perplexing stare.

"What could we do?" she asked. She used the Chinese word *mei banfa*—there is nothing to be done.

Sensing my frustration, she apologized for having to end early, but, she told me, no one could so much as question the system. I was telling her how angry I was at the situation, but she cut me off mid-sentence.

"You're not angry," she assured me; "you're just *disappointed*."

But the truth was that I was *angry*. Anger was always so controlled in China—there were few senseless acts of violence committed by common people—but by the same logic, it was hard for people to express their real emotions. There was too much face at stake. Any unprovoked outburst was counter to social harmony and detrimental to fostering relationships. But in that moment I couldn't censor myself: I was vengeful and out for blood.

On the way out of the cafeteria, I started telling Grant and Tyra about how I wanted to vandalize a government office or teach bad words to the students performing "Crazy English" near the flower garden.

"We should teach them how to say 'fuck the CCP,'" I shouted, raising my fist in the air. "No one should have to put up with this."

Dance parties had been originally conceived as a way to give Chinese friends and students a safe space to unwind and be free from the pressures of Chinese society. But they came to be equally as liberating for me. A few weeks without one and the overwhelming anxiety of Taigu could sometimes be too much to bear. There were few places that made me feel more at ease, more free of inhibition, and more comfortable in my own skin. But now, that pressure from Chinese society had forced its way back in, and I felt a rebellious, destructive force begin to well up inside me. It wasn't the early end to the party that really got to me; it was my failure as a leader.

"This party was supposed to be for us," I said too loudly. "Why shouldn't we make the rules?"

I could tell the others were disappointed, but not like me. Bobby and Lynn had joined us at that point, having come to *guyuan* just as the party was being dispersed. I began receiving texts from concerned students who had also showed up to the room but saw no one else inside. Evidently, I had failed as a teacher too.

"It's not like at your house," Tyra said. "We have no control over other parts of the school." She tried to quiet me down, but I wasn't having it.

"Yeah, but the school can still have control over us? It starts with a dance party, and then pretty soon they're telling us what we can eat and where we can shit." The words felt caustic as they left my lips.

Tyra shook her head disapprovingly. "Now you're just being ridiculous," she said.

"And you're being naïve," I snapped back.

"When are you going to accept," she said, her voice low and steady, "that there are some things about China that you can't change?"

I was still shouting and causing a scene all the way to North Yard. We went out to eat a late dinner of *chuan*, skewered meat and vegetables on sticks, over brimming glasses of draft beer at an outdoor restaurant. The waiter sat us down at two long, rectangular tables right next to the grated coal boxes used as a grill. The seats were tiny red plastic stools that buckled and sagged under any pressure. Across from us, a group of large men in stained wife-beaters was jauntily pounding beer steins on the table and ripping into greasy sticks of braised lamb. For a long while, we all stared at the menus in silence, and no one could bring themselves to look at me.

THERE'S
MERCURY
IN THAT
WATER,
AND YOU

It was probably when she had finished with the breasts and was moving on to the male genitalia that I really lost it.

"Don't move, or you'll ruin it," she said with a giggle. She was on all fours now, running her hands over my covered body. I was laughing too, so hard that the sand was coming loose and pooling in my underarms and the space between my thighs, exactly where she needed it to stay firm.

Tyra was an aspiring painter, but she made an exception for sand sculpture. Ever since she was little, she had loved to dig, playing with a bucket and a shovel on beach outings with her family all the way up until middle school. Tyra told me once that when she finally decided she was too old for it, her mom clutched her chest and fixed her with a look that embodied the whole of growing up, as if to say, *but this is what you loved.* On this trip, Tyra was tapping into that past, and I agreed to be her canvas.

Prostrate, I waited as she fashioned a new body for me. Originally, I was supposed to be this muscular bodybuilder—a professional wrestler entombed in tawny sand. My head was tilted just far down enough that I could make out the bulging arms and the chiseled abdomen that she had created with only her hands. Later, she found it to be too boring and started in with these huge sagging breasts that spilled over into my arms when I laughed. Then she got to work on a gigantic penis that pointed straight down from between my thighs like a water cannon.

A few other tourists walked by and flashed us these radiant smiles—giving a thumbs up and a curious grin to the artist. I was just glad that we were foreigners at a fancy resort in Bali, which as far as I was concerned was license enough to do whatever we pleased.

After over a month of backpacking and trekking together in Southeast Asia, this was a well-deserved vacation: three days on the Indonesian island of Bali. We knew that what we wanted would be pricey, and despite scrimping on cheap hostels and street food every step of the way to get there, we weren't prepared for the 100 dollar per night price tag at most of the boutique hotels up along the coast. Finally, Tyra's uncle, Rick, offered to pony up the money. He was a New York City lawyer and wanted to give Tyra a birthday gift that he knew she would appreciate.

The beach wasn't at all what we expected. The guidebooks indicated that it was a lush, uninhabited oasis, but when we arrived, the sand was littered with wide beach chairs and pointy umbrellas, which could have passed for the Jersey shore. The beach was actually called Sanur, but I had originally thought the area was "Snore," a misunderstanding I didn't think would prove to be prophetic. The resort was inhabited by what appeared to be an entire community of overweight, recumbent retirees. It was as if no one under the age of 45 was granted entry.

Tyra and I saw them in all of their various natural states—ballooned lopsidedly over two borrowed towels, galumphing clumsily up from the surf, pouches sagging and protruding out from under their too-tight tops. Some of the women were sunbathing nude, their flattened, leathery skin glistening in the late afternoon sun. I remembered the word *kong long*—dinosaur, in Chinese—that was used as slang to describe undesirables, and held my tongue.

We pulled up along a comparatively emptier patch of sand. Tyra applied another layer of sunscreen while perched atop one of the many beach chairs. Already her skin was pink like the gills of a salmon, but she was not red yet, and Tyra was nothing if not persistent.

"Not today," she muttered as she took another white globule and painted it in wide streaks across her neck and shoulders. She handed the plastic tube to me, and I took a small amount, dabbing the outside of my ears and my nose. Mostly I just wanted to be polite.

"I'm so jealous of your skin," she said lightheartedly, sliding her hands along her collarbone and down over the tops of her freckled breasts. She joked that even on the rare occasions when I burned, the redness would last one day and then gradually recede into a dark tan without peeling. "But you really are going to get skin cancer if you're not careful," she said. "You know every time you tan, you're killing skin cells, right?" My skin was just the beginning. I had a bad habit of eating raw street food and not fully boiling my water.

I rolled my eyes. "Yeah, yeah," I said jokingly, as I handed back the sunscreen.

Tyra was wearing a black two-piece bikini with a clasp that fastened in a ring in the front and two ties that wrapped around her neck. Her waist cut this dramatic crease down the side as it met with her hips. Meanwhile, my body was sticky and itchy from the sand. Already, it was rubbing against my forearms and my skin was radiating pink. I pressed my fingers to my skin, watching it turn white for a brief moment before fading back to a pale red. I turned my gaze outward and thought about the entire ocean encircling us.

"What are we still doing on land?" I asked, getting up. I dusted some of the sand off instinctively from my abdomen; I couldn't wait to get in the water. "How about one more swim before dinner?" The sun was beginning to get low in the sky, and I was hungry but could wait. I held my hand out to Tyra and pulled her up. We galloped full tilt toward the water, and it was only after I dove in, submerging my entire body under water and reemerged, that I saw Tyra's pace slow to a trot. She was taking calculated steps, waiting as each wave lashed against her thighs before making another track inwards.

I saw an opening, and I seized it. Without warning, I doubled back to Tyra and tackled her into the water. As she broke the surface, she let out a thin shriek and landed soft blows against my chest. "No fair," she protested, using the whiny voice that we both loved to make fun of. We heard it all the time in Taigu from Chinese girls who made their boyfriends hold their purses or bags for them and then railed on them when they did something wrong. "*Wo tao yan ni*"—"I hate you"—they'd scream, like bratty teenagers in America who pouted and kvetched when things didn't go their way.

Tyra jumped into my arms and wrapped her legs tightly around my waist. I snatched her up—pressing her body against mine—and waded out in the water until my thighs were fully submerged. I stepped over the murky seaweed, managing to stub my toes on the rocky crags that jutted out from the ocean floor. With each step, she swung from side to side as I tried hard to keep my balance.

"I wonder what's down there," she said, resting her head casually in the space between my chest and my chin.

"Where?" I asked, haphazardly scooting around a clump of muddy brambles.

"You know, the water," she said. "I wonder what's in it." She looked around anxiously. "Do you think there are any sharks out there?"

The water was as warm as a bath, and was teeming with plankton. Further afield, I squinted and made out a small family of fish scampering back and forth among the dead coral.

"Probably just mercury," I said, the sentence muddled and clumsy in my throat. I didn't know why it suddenly came to me. I remembered reading somewhere that levels of mercury in the Pacific Ocean had nearly doubled in the last decade and were climbing even higher. Most experts were attributing it to runoff from Chinese coal plants, which were some of the biggest polluters on the continent. Still, compared to Chinese water, the Bali surf looked stunningly, impossibly clean.

I slowed my pace, staring down at the swirl of blue and white at my feet. In China, there were reports of street vendors using filtered gutter oil—*di gou you*—to save money on cooking oil. Then there was melanin in baby formula, contaminated fish kept in raw sewage before being sold, urine in the milk, opiate in the hot pot. Concerned students even warned against drinking *nai cha,* our beloved bubble tea, because of fear of glue in the tapioca balls. Some Chinese friends stopped eating in North Yard altogether because of it. I kept eating there anyway, not wanting to find out what was safe and what wasn't.

I put Tyra back down in the water, and we swam around on our own for a time. I did a couple of laps away from the shore. After I felt I had gone far enough, I let the ocean carry me back, with my chest to the sky and my arms paddling lightly at my sides. I had my head tilted back against the current and was drifting along in the water, slowly counting my breaths.

When we came back together, Tyra wanted me to try grabbing her by the waist and hoisting her up over my head like in a dance move she had seen in *Dirty Dancing.* I had never seen the movie myself, but I enjoyed the challenge, trying to time it right so that when she jumped she didn't accidently knee me in the face as her body shot up from the water. Her waist was smooth and slippery in my hands, and when I caught her in the air for each fleeting moment before she slid from my grasp, I wondered what it might be like to hold her just a second longer.

We were both starving and the sun was beginning to set, so we hoisted ourselves out of the clear water and back onto land. Nearly all of the beachgoers had left, and the remnants of empty beach chairs and half-drunk banana daiquiris looked like a cynical rendering of the world after humans. We walked back up to our hotel. Outside was a little bar and grill that the hotel staffed with small tables and lit by candlelight. Without going back home to change, we took our seats facing the ocean and eyed the menus.

It was a beautiful night, and a cool breeze was blowing fitfully against my exposed back and chest. Ten-foot-tall palm trees adjoined the hotel and restaurant. They jutted up from the sand and acted like canopies to block out the moon. There were strings of paper lanterns running between the trees, tiny decorative triangles that bounced and glided with the wind. Tyra wrapped herself in a shawl that dipped like a hammock between her shoulders.

From the menu, I ordered a burger with fries and a large banana milkshake. We had been eating locally everywhere we went, and I had always been wary of local interpretations of foreign food, but this place catered to Westerners, and pretty soon, I wouldn't be able to find Western food at all again anymore. *It's my damn vacation*, I thought, *and I can order whatever I want.*

Tyra and I had always disagreed about Western food in China. Whereas I took it where I could find it, she prided herself on only ever really wanting to eat Chinese food. I was convinced that three months into living in Taigu she would crack, but she stayed firm and only caved whenever the other foreigners insisted on going out to a Western restaurant when we traveled. I lost a bet because of it—and had to give up eating white rice for a week—which nearly killed me. It was one of our few points of contention. But here, she made an exception, and ordered a burger too. They came out in these sterling white dishes—the burger glistening, the fries dancing off the plate. I felt like it was the first time I'd laid my eyes on one.

I started in on my burger like a famished animal. The whole time I was eating, Tyra kept giving me these darting, furtive looks, catching my eye, and then just as quickly turning away. She loved the way I ate anything. She told me that watching me enjoy something that much gave her a great deal of pleasure too. I leaned back in the wooden chair, mesmerized by the smell of the ocean, the soft call of the night air.

"I have to tell you something…" Tyra said, her sentence trailing off. "I mean, I *want* to tell you something." She cowered and fussed with her hair—stringy and wet from the water.

"It's just that…" She flashed me this bashful smile, her face turning rosy at the cheeks. I leaned in close to her, making her even more skittish. She looked at me with those big, blue eyes that stayed half-open even when she slept.

"Never mind," she said finally. "It's nothing, really." She looked up at me and back down at the burger on her plate. "I'll save it for another time."

In a few days, we would be leaving to go back to Taigu for my last four months. A part of me was excited to go back—tired of the constant packing and moving and living out of a backpack, and ready to settle into a routine. But I knew that another part would miss this moment—of being exactly where I was in life, and of sharing it with Tyra. We traveled better together than anyone else I had ever met. And I knew, somewhere deep down, that I might never in my life have a trip quite like this again.

I could guess exactly what she was thinking, what she yearned desperately to say. But I fixed her with a playful grin that tried to feign ignorance as much as possible—like I didn't have any idea. The truth was that the thought had crossed my mind too—more than once. But I didn't think I was ready. I thought about where I was the previous winter, traveling with Rachel, and it all felt too close. What if the two had simply switched places in my consciousness? I wondered if there would always be something lingering, deep and intractable, underneath the surface, or if there was something else in that water, just waiting to be discovered.

I stood up from my chair and started towards the bathroom, running my fingers through my hair. I passed through the hotel's lobby, outfitted with marble-tiled floors and aged oak chairs, and into the atrium that opened up to the sky. I paused and held my hands out in front of me. It was a full moon, and the light cast a soft glow over my entire body. My skin felt smooth and tranquil, and for a brief moment I thought I could see right through it. My eyes moved from my palms to my fingertips. I hadn't even noticed them earlier. My fingernails were a milky pink—sparkling and pure; they'd never looked so bright.

LEAVING

Most Fellows find that getting ready to leave is difficult. In the short time it takes to travel back to the U.S.A., the new life you have struggled to build will disappear. Friends and familiar routines will be left behind. No doubt there will be regrets: language left unperfected, opportunities for friendship left unplumbed, places yet unvisited.

TO THE LOSERS
GO THE SPOILS

At 7:00 AM, I got a call from the office. They only called us when there was a problem at the school or when there was a banquet we needed to attend, and always did so at the most inopportune times. I hung up the phone, walked across the living room, and knocked loudly on Grant's door. There was a problem at the school.

As a result of not passing the foreign teacher-taught oral English classes over the last year, just about 60 graduate and doctoral students were in danger of flunking out of Shanxi Agricultural University. The students had all failed our classes for a variety of reasons. Some had plainly never once attended class. Others had come for one or two classes before deciding to stop altogether. Others had taken a leave of absence after finding employment in another city or county. Still others never took the final exam either of their own volition or because of our mandates prohibiting students who had missed a certain percentage of classes from doing so. Regardless, school policy stated that if a student failed even one class, he or she would not be eligible to receive a diploma.

From a Western educational perspective, this would not have been so great a problem. After all, it was the student's individual choice that had resulted in a failing grade; it wasn't the fault of the university. But from a Chinese point of view, this was a big problem indeed. After all, if of the 380 or so students who matriculated every year in graduate school, 60 were not graduating, that was over 15 percent who weren't getting their degrees. This not only reflected badly on the university but also served as a warning for prospective students that they only stood an 85 percent chance of graduating. Like most of the cultural conflicts we Westerners came across in China, this too was a matter of "face." In other words, a poor graduation rate brought down a school's credibility and effectively discouraged new students from applying.

In order for those students not to fail, our bosses—Zhao Huang and Xiao Yin—told us, the students would all have a retest. That retest, in the form of a written essay in English, would come on a Sunday following two days of classes—two on Friday and two on Saturday, each for two hours. The classes were scheduled to be taught, we soon learned, by Grant and me, as well as a Chinese English professor—with Grant and I splitting Friday classes and the other teacher taking the Saturday ones. The business of administering the final exam and the grading would also fall to the two of us.

Grant and I were flatly appalled. The administration was essentially telling us that coming to four classes and taking a makeshift final exam was all it took to pass oral English at Shanxi Agricultural University. It seemed that instead of condemning bad students, the administration was actually endorsing their bad behavior—doing everything in its power to help them to succeed. It was ironic, considering that the road leading up to attending college in China is paved with sleepless nights of manic studying. College itself, by comparison, is a breeze, and Chinese students have a reputation for getting lazier with each subsequent degree they earn. Students routinely skipped classes that they found boring, texted in the back of crowded lecture rooms, and played Warcraft in smoky internet bars in lieu of doing homework.

It was easy to pin the blame on the Foreign Affairs Office. After all, they were the ones approaching us about the issue and offering what in their minds was a plausible alternative. But even our boss Zhao Huang had her misgivings. When we asked about the content of those classes, she simply smiled and laughed.

"Anything," she told us in Chinese. "You can even berate the class for the entire two hours for all I care."

It would have been an easier pill to swallow had the Foreign Affairs Office taken a more lenient approach to disciplinary enforcement in the past. Quite the contrary, Zhao Huang was our biggest advocate the previous semester when it came to failing the scores of students who had only in the last week started coming to our classes. She assured us that this wasn't an easy decision. With one or two failing students, it wouldn't have been a problem, but 60 was too many to ignore. Under pressure from her higher-ups, she relented, even as she recognized that it wasn't fair— both to us and to the dozens of students who actually deserved the grades they had received. But ultimately, as was so often the case in China, there was nothing she could do to change it.

It felt like all of our conventional Western wisdom—that those who work hard are rewarded, and that those who don't are punished—had been turned on its head. In fact, the very act of "failing" a student may have been a totally Western concept. Other departments at the school didn't have this problem—even students who never once showed up to class were still buoyed by the Chinese education system. It might have explained how we had students in our classes who had taken over ten years of English and could still barely read the alphabet. Grant left for Beijing that weekend, so it was up to my guilty conscience to eventually suck up my pride and acquiesce.

On Friday morning, I felt like I had walked into a cold, dead place. On the front door, a crude bolt-lock opened up to a room full of lethargic spirits and dull, blank stares. The classroom looked like the kind of place where learning went to die. The lighting seemed ghostly and hollow, the arrangement of the desks felt entirely impersonal, and the drywall paneling had yellowed with age. Weathered photographs of Mao paired with inspirational quotes lined each of the four walls. The teaching building directly overlooked North Yard, and all of the honking, shouting, and loud music from the street wafted its way up to my classroom, even with the windows closed. I felt like I could have been entering a rehab facility for dropouts and delinquents—it was clear that *no one*, myself and my boss included, had any desire to be there.

My boss was the first to address the class. Generally a mild-mannered and sweet woman, Zhao Huang never sounded fiercer. She bluntly told the class of flunkouts that they were there because of school policy and not because they deserved a second chance. She herself commented on the injustice of how coming to four classes was not a substitute for an entire year's worth of English classes and talked at length about the enormous opportunity that they had wasted: the chance to take English classes with actual Americans—an opportunity that other, perhaps more motivated, students would have killed for. At the end of her spiel, she took attendance—a regulation, she told me earlier, of assessing that the students were at least capable of attending *any* class—before gracefully exiting and handing the floor over to me.

In truth, I was much more nervous about teaching this class than I was about my own. Zhao Huang had originally wanted Grant and me to teach because we would at least have had some interaction with the students. After all, they were students who had had Nate, Rachel, Jerry, Darren, Grant and I as teachers last year, so our faces would at least have been recognizable to them. The downside was that I was once again face-to-face with the dozen or so students that I had personally failed, as well as dozens more who were in a similar predicament. It was like being a judge and getting put in the slammer right alongside the criminals that you were responsible for convicting. Even more, most of the students I didn't recognize were significantly older—local politicians and businesspeople who had careers and lives outside of graduate school—who were probably looking at me and wondering who this youngster was and why they should give a damn.

Still, I had listened to and lectured on Martin Luther King, Jr.'s iconic 1963 "I Have a Dream" speech with all three of my classes of graduate students that week and was feeling confident. I started class by asking in Chinese who among them could speak English. Seeing as how my good students had a hard enough time participating, I wasn't surprised when no one raised their hands. So I asked them again. Still, nothing. I decided to be a little cruel.

"It's no wonder none of you can speak English," I told them in Chinese. "Perhaps you would have if you had come to class last year." It was then that I decided to teach the class entirely in Chinese. I said that they had already wasted enough of my time coming in to teach on my day off, but that I was going to do them the favor of not requiring them to have to decipher my spoken English. I wrote a single statement on the blackboard. In all capital letters, it read: *WRITING EXERCISE: GIVE THE REASONS WHY YOU DID NOT COME TO CLASS LAST YEAR.* And while they wrote for thirty minutes, I sat reading *Blink*, and finished class by listening to each of them stand up and recite their alibis.

A part of me wanted to humiliate them, because I, too, had been humiliated. When I had failed these students in the first place, I did so with the strength and conviction of the Foreign Affairs Office behind me. I rested on a moral high ground despite those students' attempts to win me over using a combination of guilt, excuses, and bribes. And yet in spite of all of it, here I was, six months later: the only result of having put my foot down was in making more work for myself.

For my second class, I had them write on a slightly more benign topic: *What makes a good student?* At lunch, Tyra talked me down from my original writing prompt: *WRITING EXERCISE #2: WHY DO YOU THINK YOU DESERVE TO PASS THIS CLASS?* I was clutching my chopsticks over a bowl of noodle soup, shaking with anger. I told her that I was genuinely curious to hear their answers.

"How could they possibly believe that they had the right to pass oral English without having come to class?" Sensing how worked up I was getting, she reminded me not to take it personally.

"Irresponsible students make headaches for teachers across all disciplines," she told me. "This was not a problem unique to us as English teachers." She encouraged me to give them my "nothing" as anything approaching my "all" would have been far more than they deserved.

That afternoon, I was decidedly more hands-off. No more vexation boring its way under my skin, no more fuming in front of the class as I tried to appear indifferent while I read my book. Instead, I was a pale drone of myself—stern, robotic, and emotionless. For that hour of my life, it felt odd to abandon everything that I'd ever learned about teaching. I made no attempt whatsoever to pretend that I was enjoying myself or give them the slightest satisfaction. There was no excitement about the English language or praising them for good work. I was past the point of empathy. These students were slackers and good-for-nothings, and there was nothing that they could possibly learn in two days that would make up for a year's worth of careful lesson planning and dedicated teaching.

The reasons they gave for missing class were largely predictable. Most were a combination of having to do a research project or an experiment in another city, working a full-time job, taking care of aging parents, newborn children, or a sick wife, being sick themselves, or just being so bad at English that they felt that simply being in class was a waste of their time. All of them spoke at some length about how sorry they were, their obligation to their own education, and how thankful they were for the make-up classes to improve their oral English. Similar were their stock responses to the question of what makes a "good student": a person who tries their best, helps others, is respectful of their teachers, is hard-working, does their homework, goes to class, is responsible, has a "burning desire to learn," and "does everything possible to achieve their goals." Most, if not all, were probably educational propaganda slogans drilled into their heads when they were young. Few, if any, seemed to pick up on the overt irony of the question being aimed as a direct attack at their own ineptitude as graduate students.

Their English levels were actually better than I expected. Most pronounced their words clearly and their accents were comprehensible enough that I didn't struggle to understand them. No more was this true than for the girl sitting in the front row. Whereas all of the other students sat as close to the back wall as possible, she sat alone, dead center in the front of the classroom. She wore glasses, thigh-high rhinestone-studded boots, and a brown sweatshirt. A thick coif of her hair swooped seductively over her right eye. When I asked her for the reasons why she missed class, she said that she had been traveling and meeting friends in other cities. After college, it was hard to keep in touch with old classmates and there was nothing going on in Taigu anyway. She told me that class was boring and that she thought she could get away with not going. Still, she wrote, it wasn't fair to Grant, to her other classmates, to the school, or to me. She lamented the lost time and the wasted opportunity, and when I looked hard at her, I almost thought I could see her cry.

In that moment, I wanted to take everything back—the frustration and moral outrage, the feelings of humiliation and abandonment. Hearing her story, it almost made me want to forgive her right then and there. It seemed clear to me that this was just an honest girl who had made an honest mistake. And whereas few students took responsibility for their actions in their essays, she plainly did, and actually seemed to feel badly about it. There was no fabrication or rationalization. She understood that what she did was wrong and was repenting, so who was I to punish her further? I thanked her for reading and after she sat down, I fought my way through the next fourteen essays with a resolve so strong that, by the time I dismissed class, I felt like my body would crumble beneath me.

One of the other female students approached me on my way home after class. I had intentionally left the classroom a little later to avoid bumping into anyone, but apparently she had been wise to my evasion. She was unimaginably cheery, a perfect counterpoint to my moodiness. Tripping over English phrases and switching intermittently into Chinese, she began asking me some of the basic questions reserved for first-time encounters. But I had no intention of making polite conversation. Rather, I wanted to lock myself in my room and never have to think about those failing students again.

Perhaps sensing my disinterest, she worked her way in front of me and slowed me in my path. Finally, she stammered out, "I hope that we can still be friends." I thought for a moment, letting a deep breath rise slowly in my chest and exit through my lips.

I turned to her and asked in Chinese, "Who was your foreign teacher last year?" She paused for a minute.

"Actually," she told me, "I can't quite remember."

A METAPHOR
FOR SOMETHING

Sooner or later, all of the foreigners picked up new names from their Chinese students. It didn't matter whether we liked it or not—a name was a name, and we decided it was best to get used to it. Grant was "the big one," Tyra, "the beautiful one," Jerry, "the Korean one," Raina, "the one who couldn't speak Chinese," and Dylan, "the one who looked like Harry Potter." For two years, I was "the handsome one." I mention this not to brag, but because it's important for everything that happened afterwards.

Two weeks before I would leave Taigu for good, we were having a routine Chinese night at the house. The CET-6 wasn't for another week, which meant that a lot of our friends and students showed up in lieu of actually preparing for the test. On our way back home from dinner, Grant picked up the 35 *kuai* keg of beer from the *dongbei* restaurant just past the gate. Every week we'd switch off buying duties— forking over the five or six bucks that it cost to keep a party flush. The shops didn't typically sell kegs to go because they were worried that they would never get them back. But we were exceptions—given who we were, it seemed impossible that they wouldn't be able to track us down.

Draft beer and warm nights were the best parts about that summer. We'd hoist the living room couch out past the screen door and park it on the front porch next to a couple of free standing armchairs and some folding chairs we'd borrow from Jerry's house. Sometimes Dylan would play Big Joe Turner or T-Bone Walker over his speakers, and we'd just sit out there drinking for as late as we could without thinking about class the next day or going to sleep or how pretty soon we wouldn't be able to sit and drink like that together anymore.

That night, I was washing out cups in the kitchen. We would get into a bad habit of having a party and spilling beer all over the place and waiting until the start of the next party to clean it up. Our house never got too dirty, which I guess meant that we were always entertaining people.

There was a knock at the door, and I went outside to have a look. It was only 7:50; the first-timers were easy to spot because they were early. They brought with them a few bags of snacks, most just regular stuff from the *xiaomaibu*. There were already snacks—always too many—that we kept stored in a large plastic container with a latch so the rats couldn't get to them. Most of them we kept serving each week until they ran out, but the undesirables almost never left—packaged chicken feet, off-brand chocolate wafers, dried fish strips. We went and bought some good ones specially since it was our last party. Grant pulled the round table out from the kitchen, and we quickly arranged the tall stacks of chips, crinkly rice crackers, and lush packages of Oreos.

Pretty soon both the front porch and the inside of the house were jammed—the way it would sometimes get during a good dance party. A long line of students stretched from the front door down the dirt path to where it intersected with the road. It was a lot more people than usually came out, but other than that, not much was different. Like the dance parties, we had perfected the art of Chinese night so well that even though this was the last time, almost nothing strayed from the norm.

Friends came and lingered outside or gathered by the snacks. Some of them played slaps on our flimsy coffee table, shouting and hollering when they won. A couple of acquaintances wanted pictures, photo documentation, so when they showed their friends weeks and months after we had left, they could prove that we were real, that they had been in the presence of living, breathing foreigners.

No one seemed to grasp the gravity of the situation. Conversation centered around familiar topics, classes, work, movies, experiments, and it didn't seem at all like this was the *last* of anything—it didn't suggest even the slightest hint of closure. In ten days, we would all be gone; some of us would probably never return here again in our lifetimes. The other foreigners seemed unfazed—Jerry and Dylan were talking outside, Grant was inside playing cards, and Tyra was chatting with a small handful of her students. We no longer griped that we could never get Raina to come out, even for an occasion like this. I loitered by the keg on the front porch, taking long sips from my plastic cup.

I was talking with some of my former English majors outside when I saw Susan and Melody walking up the path to the house. Melody was carrying a small red package in her hands and looked excited to see me.

"Dan," she said, wrapping her arms around me. She and Susan were wearing matching outfits—rhinestone-studded jeans and a loose-fitting top that draped over her shoulders. "We just wanted to give you this," she said, handing over the box, "but we really can't stay long."

The previous week I had helped both of them with their senior theses. I suspected that both of their papers were aided greatly by previously published work on the internet, but I agreed to edit them nonetheless. I opened up the box. Inside was a bracelet fixed with earth-toned gemstones. Some of them I could already tell were made of plastic, but others of them felt hard and weighty, the way stones should.

"It's from Tibet," she said, in Chinese. "I bought it when I went to visit with my family last month."

"Thank you," I said. "It's beautiful." I knew that they would wait there until I tried it on, so I took it out of the box and hooked it around my left wrist. In the dull glow of the porch light, it didn't actually look half bad.

"What are you going to do when you get home," Melody asked.

"I don't know," I said. "See friends, try to find a job."

"I'm sure you will find a good job," Melody said with a wink. "You're so smart."

"And handsome," Susan chimed in, quickly hiding her face behind Melody.

"*Na li, na li*"—"it's nothing," I said, the way I always did, even if I secretly believed it.

I was always getting compliments like that in Taigu. Even though it had more to do with Chinese culture than it did with me, I still reveled in the attention. It is customary to say nice things to foreigners in China, and it is done so matter-of-factly you would have no reason to question its credibility. It would be tantamount to saying that it was raining out or that such-and-such a dish was good or that there was a hen over there pecking around in the bushes.

I thanked them again and suggested that we all do dinner and karaoke the following week. It had been a long time since we had gone to KTV together. They both nodded in agreement and waved goodbye, disappearing quickly into the night. I have a tendency to put off goodbyes for as long as I can, and making impractical future dates means you can at least avoid saying that goodbye where both parties know it is really the last time they will ever see each other.

There was an opening on the couch to the right of Lynn and two other girls, and I moved quickly towards the seat. Bobby was standing next to the couch and making weird smacking noises with his lips. The girls giggled and made a motion with their hands like they disapproved. Bobby was good at stuff like that—impressions, card tricks; he always had something up his sleeve.

"Hey Dan," he said, clapping me on the shoulder. "I got something to show you."

He was breaking the only rule of Chinese night by speaking in English, but

I didn't get hung up about it. Besides, it was almost 11:00, and by now the party had thinned to just over a dozen people, many of them giving me their final hugs and goodbyes. We walked across the porch to a clearing by the screen door.

"I just saw this online," Bobby said, switching to Mandarin. "There's this new push-up technique that people are talking about." Bobby knew that I was a sucker for new workout tips.

"Instead of clapping your hands in front of you between reps," he said, "you actually clap *behind* your back and bring your hands around to the front." He demonstrated the movement standing up. "That's one repetition," he said, with a hint of arrogance. And then he added: "Strong guys can do about a dozen."

It's hard to say whether I defined my reputation or whether my reputation came to define me. The second Bobby finished explaining, I was already down on my hands and knees. The front porch felt gritty and dusty under my palms but I didn't care. Before anyone had even realized what happened, my body had left the ground, my hands were behind my back, and my chin struck first on its way back to earth, plunging itself into the cement porch like a construction drill.

There was a loud noise when it happened. I could tell that people heard it, and I suddenly felt an intense desire to disappear, to be transported to a place where no one would pay a second thought to a man lying face down on the ground. I slowly got to my feet and I could feel something trickling down from my chin. Tiny red splotches began to gather on the brick tiles and along the floor. One of the girls gasped, and Bobby rushed towards me. I tried to move away, insisting that it was my fault and that I was fine, but all Bobby could do was apologize like it was this mantra that could somehow make everything better.

Nearly everyone who was still at the house ushered me into the bathroom. Given that it was really only big enough for a couple of people, most of them just milled around outside uncomfortably, trying to sneak a look in. My body was in too much of an adrenaline shock to feel pain, but it looked serious. The gash cut into the left side of my chin nearly an inch deep and the blood was a dark crimson. Tyra located a small box of cotton swabs and Bobby ran out to grab the bottle of *baijiu* he brought for the party so that I could sterilize the wound. The alcohol sent shooting pains up and down my face but it didn't feel much worse than its normal position at the back of my throat.

Anytime Tyra or Bobby left the bathroom, someone else tried to come in, and eventually it became too much to deal with. I shooed everyone away, embarrassed that anyone had to see me at all, until finally I was the only one left. I felt blasé about the whole thing. I knew that my life wasn't in danger and that everything would be fine. But this party wasn't supposed to be about me. I shuddered to think that this would be my lasting legacy—that of all the memories we shared, this would be the one that people would remember.

I went into my bedroom and shut the door. It was muggy outside and the air was hot and sticky. I kept my two windows open and the wind ruffled the cotton blinds like they were great sails coursing through the ocean. I sat at the foot of my bed and had my head tilted back, cradling my chin with a handful of tissues. Two, maybe three minutes passed. Tyra came in and closed the door behind her.

"How does it feel? Can I get you anything?"

"It's fine," I said. "It should probably stop bleeding in a few minutes."

The music was still on in the living room and I could hear people talking from the porch through my open window. They were saying how unexpected the whole thing was, how sudden. They were looking at the streak of deep red on the cement tile outside and wondering if it would ever come off.

"I feel like this is a metaphor for something," I said.

"For what?"

"I don't know, Taigu, everything, this entire experience." I waited a moment. I shook my head to myself, almost laughing. The tissues were getting damp, so I rolled them up into a ball and threw them out. Tyra gave me a fresh set and I placed them delicately over my chin.

"You probably shouldn't do that," she said. "The paper is dirty. Dylan really thinks you should go to the hospital."

"I don't need to go to the hospital," I told her. "The bleeding should stop soon."

She was insistent, and we went back-and-forth like that for a time. All the while, I couldn't even look at her. My gaze shifted from the clot of napkins in my hand to the wooden floor beneath my feet. It struck me that all this would happen now—that everything about myself that I was ashamed of would be revealed in one last encounter with the people I had come to know—the impulsiveness, the bravado, the inability to back down. I wanted to ask myself: this notion that I was invulnerable—was it always there or did *China* give this to me? I started up again as if I had been speaking aloud the whole time.

"Everyone calling you beautiful all the time," I began. "Doesn't it get to you after a while?"

"Of course," she replied. "It does for all of us. But it sort of becomes normal and you just accept it."

"That's exactly it. People only know you from what's on the surface. And pretty soon that starts to become who you are."

She paused a moment before answering. "Only if you let it. You mean, like if you actually start believing it?"

I tilted my head back and exhaled to the ceiling. My breath was quickening. Already I could feel something welling up in my eyes. "I think I wanted to," I said, just loud enough for her to hear.

I dabbed at my chin with my left hand. I reached around the bed for more tissues but there were none left. "It's like this whole thing was a reality check," I said, louder than I expected. "Like the universe is telling me, 'When you go back to America, you will be a nobody again, just like everybody else.'"

I stood up and walked to the bathroom. I flipped on the light and caught a glimpse of my reflection in the mirror. My chin was exposed, and my eyes looked swollen and puffy. I was haunted by this feeling that I was living a charmed life, that so much of what I was experiencing wasn't *real* to the outside world—the pervasive sense that when I inevitably came back, it would all up and dissipate as if I had never left home to begin with. It was paralyzing, the thought that I could have changed so much in two years that I was a stranger to myself. And that's when I started crying.

In ten minutes, Tyra, Dylan, Bobby and I would all be in a taxi going to the hospital. I would be rattling on the whole way about how stupid everything was and how we weren't even drunk and why all of this happened to begin with. In thirty minutes, I would be sitting in a powder blue armchair while a doctor threaded a needle in and out of my exposed wound, the blood pulsing like small rivulets and pooling in a cloth at the base of my neck. In between sutures he would tell me about his daughter, how she would be a graduate student at the university that year and how he named her and her sisters after *Feng Shan*, one of these big mountain ranges in town—

the same one that on rare clear days you could see enveloping the entire campus.

I'd get seven stitches in my chin that night. The next day, everyone I talked to would already know about the incident. I would wear a thick bandage taped to the side of my face until I saw some of my students walking to lunch and took it off because I'd decide it looked too ridiculous. In six weeks, my chin would be completely healed, leaving only a small, knotted lump at the base the color and consistency of wax. I kept staring at my reflection in the mirror. I had this feeling that the longer I looked the more everything would start to make sense again. I tore off a few turns of toilet paper, wiped my nose, and shoved the rest in my pocket. Tyra knocked on the door; it was time to go. All the things you can't forget, the marks that stay with you forever.

THE END

ACKNOWLEDGEMENTS

This book would not have been possible without the tireless dedication and support of a number of important individuals. First and foremost, I want to thank Wilder Voice Press for agreeing to publish this rather unorthodox work, and everyone involved on the staff for working so hard to push this novel through to fruition. Specifically, I would like to extend a huge thanks to Sage Aronson and John West. They are a dynamic, vibrant, and awesomely talented editing team that are responsible for shaping these stories into what they are.

Professor Laurie McMillin deserves enormous credit for being such an incredible mentor throughout the writing process and for agreeing to pen my first review. I would also like to thank Deb Cocco and Carl Jacobson at Oberlin Shansi for giving me the opportunity that has forever changed my life and allowing me the freedom to write about it. Of course, no acknowledgments section would be complete without also thanking my loving family—Mom, Hannah, and especially Dad—for never once doubting that this book was possible.

Special thanks go to James Barnard, Scott Grabel, Tino Merino, Alexandra Sterman, and Alejandra Wundram, who expressed a genuine interest in my work and were gracious enough to offer insightful feedback and criticism in its early stages. The same goes for my classmates in Professor McMillin's "Writing about Travel" class who continue to be so receptive and enthusiastic about my writing. To David Brown, Nick Hatt, Gerald Lee, David Petrick, and Ben Reitz, from whom I so shamelessly solicited information and anecdotes, I also offer a big thank you.

I received a great deal of creative inspiration—though admittedly, quite indirectly—from storytelling giants both living and dead: Raymond Carver, Dan Chaon, Edwidge Danticat, Ira Glass, Peter Hessler, and David Sedaris, among others. Additional thanks go to a few intangibles: Pandora's Sigur Ros Station, Pearl Jam's "Live in Toronto," Google Docs, thesaurus.com, and the computer classroom in Mudd Library at Oberlin College. Thanks too to the countless others who offered encouragement and kind words at various stages of the novel's completion.

Lastly, I would like to thank the friends and students who I had the great privilege of getting to know over my two years in Taigu as well as the many acquaintances I met traveling throughout Asia. Thank you. Were it not for you, these stories would not exist.

Made in the USA
Middletown, DE
01 December 2016